Weeknight Grilling
with the BBQ Queens

Weeknight Grilling with the BBQ Queens

Karen Adler *and* Judith Fertig

THE HARVARD COMMON PRESS

Boston, Massachusetts

The Harvard Common Press
535 Albany Street
Boston, Massachusetts 02118
www.harvardcommonpress.com

Printed in the United States of America
Printed on acid-free paper

Library of Congress Cataloging-in-Publication Data

Adler, Karen.
  Weeknight grilling with the BBQ queens : making meals fast and fabulous
/ Karen Adler and Judith Fertig.
      p. cm.
    Includes index.
      ISBN 1-55832-313-9 (hardcover : alk. paper) — ISBN 1-55832-314-7
(pbk. : alk. paper)
    1. Barbecue cookery. 2. Quick and easy cookery. I. Fertig, Judith M.
II. Title.
TX840.B3A338 2006
641.5'784—dc22   2005023806

ISBN-13: 978-1-55832-313-1 (hardcover); 978-1-55832-314-8 (paperback)
ISBN-10: 1-55832-313-9 (hardcover); 1-55832-314-7 (paperback)

Special bulk-order discounts are available on this and other Harvard
Common Press books. Companies and organizations may purchase books
for premiums or resale, or may arrange a custom edition, by contacting the
Marketing Director at the address above.

Cover design by Night & Day Design
Cover photographs © 2006 by Brian Hagiwara
Interior design by Richard Oriolo
Illustrations by Laura Tedeschi

10 9 8 7 6 5 4 3 2 1

To our mothers,

Denise Conde and Jean Merkle,

who fed us, body and soul

Acknowledgments

As BBQ Queens, we are indebted to our royal families, fabulous friends, culinary schools, and students, who always help us taste-test or tweak a recipe. Family members have license to give our recipes the nod or the thumbs-down, which we are grateful for on both counts. Our fabulous friends gladly share a recipe here and there. While teaching at culinary schools, for example, we came up with the double baking sheet or tray method that we use for taking foods out to the grill. The enthusiasm of culinary students is contagious and keeps a twinkle in our eyes and a lilt in our steps while we prance around the kitchen (indoors or outdoors). So, with a snap of our barbecue tongs, we salute the following:

Hugs and kisses to our families, who have been so supportive, including Karen's husband Dick; mom Dee; busy sisters Nancy, Linda, and Betsy; steppies Ellen and Jill and their families; and Judith's daughter Sarah and son Nick; sister Julie and family; and parents Jack and Jean.

Friends! Fabulous "foodie" friends include everyone in our cookbook club: Dee Barwick, Elizabeth Benson, Vicki Johnson, Gayle Parnow,

Mary Pfeifer, Kathy Smith, and Roxanne Wyss. Girlfriends that we cook with on weeknights include Janet Coffey, Dianne Hogerty, Susan Jackson, Reene Jones, LuAnn Long, Donna Missimer, Anne Saroni, Debbie Simpson, Angie Stout, Tina Thomas, and Judi Walker.

Our many friends and associates in Les Dames d'Escoffier International, the International Association of Culinary Professionals, the Kansas City Barbeque Society, and Slow Foods–Kansas City have supported us in numerous ways, and we are grateful.

We want to thank the staff of the many cooking schools where we have enjoyed teaching and meeting new food friends, including Larry Oates, owner of KitchenArt in West Lafayette, Indiana; Barbara-Jo MacKintosh and her Books to Cooks store in Vancouver, British Columbia; Deb Lackey at the Dorothy Lane School of Cooking in Dayton, Ohio; Chan Patterson and the Viking Culinary Centers all across the country; Carol Tabone at Jungle Jim's Cooking School in Fairfield, Ohio; Marilyn Markel at A Southern Season in Chapel Hill, North Carolina; Kitchen Conservatory and Dierberg's in St. Louis, Missouri; Kathleen Craig and the great staff at Cooks of Crocus Hill in Minneapolis and St. Paul, Minnesota; Macy's Dadeland in Miami, Florida; Marshall Field's Culinary Studio in Chicago, Illinois; Central Market's Cooking School at various locations in Texas; Nancy Pigg at Cooks' Wares in Cincinnati, Ohio; Priscilla Barnes and her staff at Cook's Nook in McPherson, Kansas; Cook's Warehouse in Atlanta, Georgia; Sur La Table Cooking Schools throughout the United States; Kroger's at locations throughout the United States and especially in Nashville, Tennessee; Culinary Center of Kansas City in Overland Park, Kansas; Rebecca Miller at Whole Foods Market in Overland Park, Kansas; and the wonderful staff at Roth Concept Center in Lenexa, Kansas.

Of course, we want to thank everyone at The Harvard Common Press, from publisher Bruce Shaw to executive editor Valerie Cimino to P.R. experts Skye Stewart and Liza Beth—and everyone else there. Special recognition goes to our agent, Lisa Ekus, and her able staff, and to two more eagle eyes that made our book better by copyediting and proofing—Karen Levy and Mary Ann Duckers.

Lucy Ricardo and Ethel Mertz continue to be our e-mail names to each other. Even when we are swamped or deadline crazed, the thought of these two ladies keeps us laughing every day.

Thanks, everybody!

Contents

Introduction

So many meals to get on the table, so little time. Sigh. That's what we women didn't quite bargain for when we started bringing home the proverbial bacon. Now we still have to fry it up in the pan. What, more work?

All right, that's enough of the pity party. (Notice that we gave it only a short paragraph. Whining is not regal.)

The tiara-totin' BBQ Queens have come to your rescue! We are here with grill tongs in hand and a sassy attitude to match. We hereby decree that weeknight dinners can be delicious, easy, healthy, colorful, and quick! And to prove it, we have developed and taste-tested a whole new book of fresh recipes for all seasons that you can serve your family on any busy weeknight, in roughly 30 to 45 minutes. Some will take a little less time, some will take a little more time. But all are terrific.

In our previous tome, *The BBQ Queens' Big Book of Barbecue* (The Harvard Common Press, 2005), we showed readers how to grill and smoke (and plank and rotisserie and stir-grill and skewer, etc.) like girls. Now, here's a crash course on becoming a Queen of the Weeknight Grill who can get that meal on the table *right now*.

10 Ways to Become a Queen of the Weeknight Grill

1   *Think about the whole meal.* In every single recipe, we offer ideas and instructions for other dishes to complete your dinner, if necessary, so it's one-stop menu shopping. Envision the whole meal first, then shop, chop, and plop that food on the grill, then on the table.

2   *Let the grocery store salad bar be your sous chef.* Let them chop and dice or shred ingredients; you just breeze through the salad bar and put everything into containers. Use good-quality bottled or jarred products, too. (See our Time-Saving Tiara Touches and Life in the Fast Lane ideas throughout the book for even more ways to get help and make the best use of your time.) Enlist the aid of your children, significant other, or girlfriends to set the table, flip the flatbreads, or stir together a sauce in a bowl. Somehow, kitchen duty just seems more fun and less of a chore when you're grilling.

3   *Go easy on yourself.* Offer simple, uncomplicated side dishes such as fresh fruit and raw vegetables or foods that grill right along with your entrée to complement a meal. (See our You've Got Dinner! ideas for recommendations.) Or put everything into individual surprise packages (no-mess foil-packet grilling).

4   *Eat healthfully.* Aim for three servings of fruits and/or vegetables with your evening meal. Who knows what your family members have eaten at lunch? Anyone with kids knows that even if you packed good things in their lunches, that doesn't mean they actually ate those raw veggies or that red, crisp apple. Including three fruits and/or vegetables in the evening meal is easy to do if you grill meat, poultry, or fish and a vegetable, have a sauce that's also a vegetable, and then add a simple salad or fresh fruit. For a big gold star, include a whole-grain dish, such as brown rice, polenta, or whole-grain bread.

5   *Become "tray chic."* Carry all your ingredients out to the grill (and back inside) on a baking sheet or two. (The BBQ Queens started employing this method during our grilling and smoking cooking classes; now we always do this at home.) This *mise en place* or "every ingredient ready" method saves time and

keeps you focused, because you don't have to keep running back to the kitchen to fetch a missing ingredient.

6   *Befriend olive oil.* Brush foods with olive oil, then season them with salt and pepper before grilling. The foods are less likely to stick to the grill, making grilling easier and you calmer.

7   *Stoke a hot fire.* Foods grill faster over a hot fire and taste extra good.

8   *Make your sauces function as vegetables.* Why do two things when you can combine them into one? Just like the mother who told her kids they weren't eating yucky fish, they were eating "chicken of the sea," you can tell your kids, "This is not just a vegetable. This is a salsa. *Olé.*"

9   *"Grill for leftovers" is our mantra.* Get two meals out of one effort, to use either in lunches to pack for the next day or in tomorrow's dinner. We offer lots of recipes and tips for using leftover grilled goodies. If you grill once to eat twice, you can put your feet up tomorrow and read the latest issue of that magazine-that-you-subscribe-to-but-never-get-to-read while you buff your nails. Dinner's ready already.

10   *Chill out at the grill!* Sip a glass of vino, soak up that gorgeous sunset, and smell the delicious aroma of the good food headed to your table—for the people you love best in the world. Life is good.

Weeknight Grilling with the BBQ Queens

Weeknight Grilling with a Tiara Touch

Monday through Friday night dinners need not be the same old, same old. And weeknight dinners on the grill needn't be limited to burgers and hot dogs, either. Shake things up a bit! No matter what time of year, it's fun to get out of your indoor kitchen and into an outdoor frame of mind. The BBQ Queens are here to show you how.

Grilling, simply by being an outdoor cooking proposition, is one of the most social kinds of cooking. Who says you don't have time to be social during the week? Turn off the TV and bring the drinks and munchies outdoors in good weather. Even when it's cold, drizzly, or snowy, a dinner cooked on the grill is more fun and festive. Dress your table (indoors or out) with a colorful tablecloth and fill a pretty pitcher with your drink of choice. Pull up a few chairs. Breathe in the fresh air and relax. Light the fire. Have a glass of wine or an iced tea while the grill heats up. Do the last-minute preparations on your food, and you're ready to go.

For weeknight grilling, we have chosen foods that are fairly tender— chicken breasts, pork chops, pork tenderloin, steaks of all kinds, fish fillets, shellfish, ground meat, and vegetables. When the fire is hot you'll be grilling fast, and these foods cook quickly.

Grill Once, Eat Twice!

The BBQ Queens want to make sure you make the most of your time at the grill while spending as little time as is reasonable on cooking. (After all, do you want time to kick back with a cocktail, get yourself a manicure, etc.?) These foods grill soooo fast that you'll want to think ahead to dinners (or lunches) later on in the week and do two things at once. Whenever you can, grill more chicken breasts, steaks, vegetables, or shellfish than you need for one meal. Let them cool, wrap them up, and refrigerate them for what we call a "déjà vu dinner" later in the week. We offer lots of tips and recipes for second meals of salads, soups, and sandwiches to make the most out of the time you spend at the grill.

Mise en Place

Another way of making the most of your time at the grill is to employ the concept of *mise en place*, which means "everything in place." (Sounds so nice in French, doesn't it?) The term is used to describe having all of your ingredients ready to go before cooking. We take it one step further to apply this to having yourself thoroughly organized so you can move with ease from kitchen to grill and back again. To that end, we strongly recommend that you use two, or sometimes more, heavy-gauge aluminum baking sheets, stacked, to take everything out to the grill in an organized, one-trip fashion. Always place the raw food to be cooked, along with any bastes or seasonings and necessary utensils, on the top sheet. Raw meat, poultry, and fish will often be in a bowl or on a plate on top of the sheet. Always use one of the clean baking sheets to carry the cooked food to the table or kitchen counter.

Because we're BBQ Queens who like to "dine," *mise en place* also means having the table set nicely, with a simple bouquet of flowers or a potted plant for a centerpiece. Or even easier, have candles ready to light with the scratch of a match. Who says dining by candlelight is only for the weekends? Have some candles or torches outside, too. You'll feel more relaxed if you know you've got everything ready and things look nice.

Grilling over Direct and Indirect Heat

Ever wonder why restaurant food tastes so good? Why the meat is caramelized on the outside and cooked all the way through to perfection? The answer is high heat, and often that high heat comes from a grill. The BBQ Queens prefer high-heat grilling, not only for better flavor, but also for quicker meal preparation—it's perfect for a busy week.

For weeknight grilling, most of our recipes call for direct grilling, which is cooking directly over a gas or charcoal fire. Indirect grilling means you are cooking on the side of the grill away from the heat, and we offer an indirect grilling technique mainly for thick pieces of meat that are seared first, then finished on the indirect side with the lid closed. This technique also works for any food, such as bread or pizza or chicken, that you think is getting too charred for your taste. Just move it to a cooler part of the grill to finish cooking and close the lid.

Gas Grilling

The BBQ Queens recommend gas grills that have at least two or more separate burners so that you have more grilling options. With two burners, you'll be able to grill several items at once that may need different levels of heat. If you can afford it, buy a grill that is rust resistant (or get a cover for it) and has at least 36,000 BTUs. Having plenty of grilling surface also allows you to cook extra food that can be transformed into a second weeknight grilled dinner. Take a look at our Grilled Chicken Pasta with Tomatoes, Fresh Thyme, and Brine-Cured Olives (page 160) or Grilled Lobster Potato Cakes with White Wine Lemon Drizzle and Mache (page 216) for delicious examples of this.

Of course, the great time-saving feature of a gas grill is starting the fire. To turn it on, you simply open the gas valve and flip a switch.

Charcoal Grilling

We like charcoal grills with lids so that we have the option of grilling directly or indirectly. If you grill a lot or entertain and grill, then you may want a large cooking surface. If you're in a small apartment or are just cooking for two, then you can go as small as a hibachi grill. With charcoal, you get great flavor in your food. In fact, there are multi-fuel grills designed to use both gas and charcoal, so you get ease of use but don't miss out on that charcoal flavor. Charcoal fires take longer to start, so take this into account for your weeknight grilling timetable. For a tiara touch, use hardwood lump charcoal, which is irregularly shaped and made only from hardwoods. It burns as hot as Hades and is all-natural, with no added chemicals. The BBQ Queens like that!

Electric, Wood Pellet, and Kamado Grilling

Electric grills are available for indoor and outdoor use. The heat level of these grills varies greatly, so make sure you buy a unit that gets hot enough to sear. An electric grill is ideal for small patio homes and apartments where gas and charcoal models are often prohibited. One of the most popular indoor and outdoor electric grills is the George Foreman. Its heating elements are on both sides of the grill, and they cook the food extremely quickly without its having to be turned.

Wood pellet grills combine the ease of an electric starter with the flavor of compressed wood pellets. The grill needs to be plugged into an electrical outlet outdoors, then you add wood pellets to the hopper, where they're fed down a chute to the electric ignition to burn and smoke. The wood pellets are compressed, so they take up much less storage room than charcoal does, and they impart a wonderful wood flavor to all of the food you cook. For a tiara touch, buy several different flavors of wood pellets and mix and match for your own custom wood flavor.

Several basic tools make grilling easier. Kitchen shops, hardware stores, restaurant supply stores, and barbecue and grill retailers will be good sources for finding the items listed. Professional utensils are superior in quality and durability. Remember that long handles are preferable on everything, to keep you a safe distance from the fire.

- **A stiff wire brush with a scraper makes cleaning the grill a simple job (tackle this while the grill is still warm).**

- **A natural-bristle basting brush is used to apply oil to the grill grates; use a second brush to baste food during grilling or smoking.**

- **Grate Chef Grill Wipes are small pads saturated with high-temperature cooking oil. They are great for oiling the grill grates prior to cooking. Then turn them over to clean off the grill when you're finished cooking. The high-temperature oil doesn't get smoky, and the oil doesn't drip from the pads, preventing flare-ups.**

- **Perforated grill racks go on top of the grill grates to accommodate small or delicate food items, such as chicken wings, fish fillets, scallops, shrimp, and vegetables, that might fall through the wider grill grates.**

- **Grill woks or metal-shaped baskets with perforated holes sit directly on top of the grill and let in smoky flavor. Stir-grill small tender cuts of meat, fish, shellfish, and vegetables by tossing with long-handled wooden paddles. Always oil the grill rack and woks on both sides before using so that food won't stick and cleanup will be easy.**

- **Heat-resistant oven or grill mitts offer the best hand protection, especially when you need to touch any hot metals during the grilling process.**

- **Long-handled spring-loaded tongs are great for turning steaks, chops, tenderloins, shrimp, scallops, sliced vegetables, and skewers.**

- Long-handled offset spatulas with an extra-long spatula surface are great for turning large pieces of food and more delicate items that can't be turned with tongs, such as fish fillets and burgers.

- A spray bottle or pan filled with water is handy to douse flare-ups.

- Skewers—wooden or metal—allow smaller items to be threaded loosely together and then placed on the grill to cook. Wooden or bamboo skewers should be soaked for 30 minutes before using so the ends won't char during grilling (take that extra time into account when planning your weeknight grilling).

- Disposable aluminum pans or heavy-duty aluminum foil are used to hold meats or vegetables and their natural juices or sauces for basting. The pans can be bent and shaped to fit in a small grill, and the foil can be shaped into packets. Fast weeknight cleanup is just a trash can away.

- Professional baking sheets are great for many uses, including carrying food and other items back and forth from kitchen to grill. We recommend buying half-sheet baking pans made from heavy-gauge, professional-weight aluminum that resists warping. They will last a long time.

- Thermometers tell you when meat is properly cooked. We like instant-read meat thermometers.

- A charcoal chimney or an electric fire starter makes starting a charcoal fire a lot easier.

- A good-quality chef's knife is indispensable for any kind of chopping and for slicing meat.

The kamado porcelain cooker is an Asian-style cooker shaped like an egg, similar to ancient clay vessels such as tandooris. The kamados are very heavy and are usually sold with either a metal base on wheels or a heavy-duty wooden cart with wheels. When the lid is clamped shut, it cooks like a pressure cooker, more quickly than a regular smoker, and with the lid open it works well as a grill.

Lighting the Fire

Charcoal fires can be started in several safe, ecologically sound ways. The BBQ Queens prefer using real hardwood lump charcoal instead of compressed charcoal briquettes. It gives a better flavor to your food and is an all-natural product without chemical additives.

To light a charcoal fire, completely fill a metal charcoal chimney (an upright cylindrical metal canister that looks like a large metal coffee can with a handle) with hardwood lump charcoal. Place the chimney on a nonflammable surface, such as concrete or the grill rack. Slightly tip the chimney over and stuff one or two sheets of crumpled newspaper into the convex-shaped bottom. Light the paper with a match. After about 15 minutes, the coals will be hot and starting to ash over, signaling that you can get a hot fire going. Be sure to check it after the first 5 minutes to make sure the charcoal has caught fire, or you may need to light another piece of newspaper (this is from the voice of experience). When the coals are red hot in the middle and completely ashed over, dump the hot coals into your grill and add more unlit charcoal to the grill, if necessary.

Other fire starters we recommend are an electric fire starter and solid fire starters made with paraffin (see the manufacturer's directions). Start a charcoal grill 20 to 30 minutes before you're ready to grill.

To start a gas grill, follow your manufacturer's directions, because there are differences in how the burners work on the many models that are available. Most simply, you open the gas valve, then turn on the grill switch or switches to light the fire. Most models have thermometers attached to the lid, so it is easy to see when your fire is at 300°F for a medium fire and 450°F and above for a searing hot fire. Start a gas grill 10 to 15 minutes before you're ready to grill. The older the grill, the longer it takes to heat up.

The Hand Method for Judging a Grill's Temperature

Hold your hand 5 inches above the heat source. If you can hold it there for only about 2 seconds, your fire is hot (about 450°F or more); 3 seconds is a medium-hot fire (about 400°F); 4 seconds is a medium fire (about 300°F).

Adjusting Your Grill's Temperature

On a charcoal grill, always begin the fire with the bottom or side vents open. Lower the temperature by slightly closing the vents, and raise the temperature by opening the vents or by adding more charcoal. More air means the fire will burn faster and hotter while less air means the fire will burn lower and slower.

On a gas grill, adjust the heat by turning the heat control knobs to the desired level. Although some gas grill control knobs are marked only "high" and "low," there is a full range of flame heights available. On some models, you can control the temperature by turning the temperature dial.

How to Grill

Once the grill grates have been oiled to prevent the food from sticking and your grill is at the proper temperature for the recipe, just place the food on the hot grill grate. Let it sear and char slightly to get good grill marks before turning it with grill tongs or a grill spatula. We prefer not to use a grill fork, because it pokes holes in the food and lets the juices run out, resulting in drier food.

Specialty Weeknight Grilling Techniques

Grilling foods over a hot fire will give you a fast and fabulous meal. (Or two meals, if you plan ahead and employ our grill once, eat twice philosophy!) But sometimes, you want to change things up a bit. Women, in general, and the BBQ Queens in particular, don't subscribe to the "If it ain't broke, don't fix it"

When you grill, it's usually smaller, thinner cuts of meat cooking fast and hot. We prefer a hot fire, around 450°F, for most of our grilled foods because we like a little char. If you don't, then cook on a medium to medium-hot fire and increase the cooking times below to allow at least 2 to 3 minutes more. We recommend turning meats and fish once, halfway through the cooking time.

Burgers (¹/₂ inch thick)	**8 minutes for rare**
Beefsteak (I inch thick)	**8 minutes for rare**
Chicken breast paillard (I inch thick)	**5 minutes for done**
Turkey steak (¹/₂ inch thick)	**8 to 10 minutes over medium-hot fire**
Fish fillets or steaks (5 to 8 ounces)	**10 minutes per inch of thickness**
Swordfish, tuna, and other meaty fish	**7 to 8 minutes per inch of thickness**
Pork loin or rib chops (I inch thick)	**8 minutes for rare**
Pork tenderloin (2 inches thick)	**12 to 15 minutes for rare**

rule. We like change for change's sake. Something different. That's why we've offered a few specialty grilling techniques that are also fast and fabulous for your busy week.

Weeknight Skewering

For a real tiara touch, nothing beats threading foods onto a skewer to sizzle deliciously and attractively on the grill, for a meal that looks good as well as tastes good. (Like most women, we like to accomplish two things at once!) You can use just about any "stick" as a skewer, from the basic backyard campfire stick to the inexpensive bamboo you find at the grocery store to fancy metal skewers.

GRILLING TEMPERATURE TABLE

Burgers	125°F rare, 140°F medium, 160°F well done
Beefsteak	125°F rare, 140°F medium, 160°F well done
Chicken breast	160°F
Turkey breast	160°F
Fish fillets or steaks	Begins to flake when tested with a fork in thickest part
Shellfish	Opaque and somewhat firm to the touch
Pork tenderloin and chops	125°F rare, 140°F medium, 160°F well done

For a diamond-studded tiara touch, use spikes of fresh sugar cane or fresh rosemary branches. Wooden skewers need to be soaked in cold water for at least 30 minutes before threading them with food and grilling. Fresh herb or metal skewers don't need pretreatment.

After grilling, you just throw the charred skewers away. Reusable metal skewers, preferably flat rather than round so that food won't twirl around on them as easily, or the new metal coil skewers, can be easily cleaned with soapy water, then towel dried so they don't get water spots.

We've found that the best way to make sure all your food gets done at the same time is to avoid those '50s-style kabobs, with meat and vegetables all on one stick. We think it's better to have all vegetables, all meat, all fish, or all fruit on one stick, so everything gets done to a turn and you don't have a wilted, charred cherry tomato next to a springy, bloody chunk of beef. Leave about $1/8$ inch of space between foods on a skewer. If the pieces of chicken or fish are squashed together, that inside part where the pieces touch will not get done as quickly.

When you grill skewers, place them perpendicular to the grill grates and turn them with grill tongs. If you're really worried about your food falling though the

The BBQ Queens go for a bit of wood smoke while we're grilling. If you like a kiss of smoke, too, then read on. Hardwoods such as alder, cedar, hickory, maple, mesquite, pecan, black walnut, oak, sassafras, and fruit woods give grilled food a range of tastes. It's fun to experiment with different woods to give a hint of smoky flavor. A word of caution: do not use resinous or sappy woods, including pine. You can buy untreated wood chips and pellets at barbecue and grill shops or from online purveyors. Other natural flora to throw on the grill for aroma include walnut or pecan shells and branches of fresh herbs such as rosemary, mint, or lemon balm. Dried corn cobs and corn husks add a sweet smokiness, too.

If the tiara touch of smoke appeals to you, here is how to do it. For a charcoal fire, soak wood chips in water for at least 30 minutes before using. Use about 1 cup and scatter them directly on the coals. In a gas grill, place dry wood chips in a heavy-duty aluminum foil packet and poke holes in the packet or place dry wood chips in a smoker box. Place the packet or box directly over the heat and let the chips smolder for about 10 minutes prior to grilling.

Wood pellets can be used with charcoal or gas grills, but they must be used dry; if you moisten them, they turn to a mushy sawdust. Make an aluminum foil packet to enclose 1/3 cup of the dry pellets, then poke holes in the packet and place directly on the coals of a charcoal fire. In a gas grill, place the packet on the grill rack over the heat. Since you don't have to soak wood pellets, they are always ready to go. Plus, they take up less storage space because they are compressed.

grates, use a kabob basket or place the skewers on a perforated grill rack, then on the grill grate.

Weeknight Foil Packet Grilling

Known by the French term *en papillote,* the method of cooking foods in a packet isn't just for the oven. A closed grill also works well to concentrate the flavors of foods as they cook in a foil packet. When you open up the packets at the dinner table—ahhhhh, what wonderful aromas and flavors. Packet grilling lets you do *three* things at once: make dinner, have easy cleanup, and enjoy wonderful, low-cost aromatherapy!

Here's how you do it. Brush olive oil onto an 18-inch square sheet of heavy-duty aluminum foil (heavy-duty foil is 18 inches wide), or spray with cooking spray, so that the food will not stick. Place any raw food that must be cooked through on the bottom layer—that usually means thin slices of meat, boneless chicken breasts, or fish fillets or steaks.

Make sure your fish, pork, chicken, or turkey is no more than 1 inch thick at its thickest part. Drizzle on a little olive oil, then season with salt and pepper. Top this layer with vegetables, such as torn leafy greens, shredded cabbage or carrots, or other fresh vegetables cut or sliced thinly or shredded so they will cook quickly. You may even add very thinly sliced potatoes seasoned with salt and pepper, either under the meat or fish or right on top of it. Spread everything out in the packet to keep it as flat as possible, so that everything cooks evenly. Drizzle with a little more olive oil. The packets will take about 14 minutes to cook at 450°F in a grill with the lid closed, so it's important to know the temperature. (If you don't have a thermometer on your grill, use the hand method described on page 9.) When in doubt, simply cook a few minutes longer. The food won't dry out because the steam and juices are captured by the foil packet.

For a tiara touch, think color, flavor, and aroma when you assemble the packets. Vegetables provide the color. Flavored butters or bold seasonings enhance the taste. Fresh herbs or Asian ingredients such as fresh ginger add aroma.

Weeknight Stir-Grilling

Stir-grilling foods in a grill wok over a hot fire is a great way to make a low-fat, one-dish meal on the grill with no mess in the kitchen! Stir-grilled meals add variety and lots of big flavor with fewer calories. Stir-grilling isn't that much different in technique than stir-frying indoors, but we think stir-grilled food tastes even better because you get that wonderful smoky, caramelized flavor from cooking outdoors on a grill.

A big joke between the BBQ Queens is that Karen is a jar freak. Karen never met a glass jar she didn't like. She saves her old jam jars and any other interesting glass containers, carefully scrubbing off the old labels and affixing her pretty gold-foil embossed stamps that say "From Karen's Kitchen." These recycled jars and bottles go out the door as gifts, filled with her spicy hot olives, a favorite BBQ Queen rub, or a delicious homemade vinaigrette. When the BBQ Queens shop for flavor-boosting pantry staples, two of our favorite brands are Alessi and Mezzetta. We especially like the pieces of black charred skin in their fire-roasted peppers. Among the jarred and bottled store-bought goodies we prize are:

- **Beer (for cooking and drinking!)**

- **Capers**

- **Fire-roasted red peppers**

- **Herbs and spices**

- **Honey**

- **Jams, jellies, and preserves**

To stir-grill, all you need is a grill wok, available at barbecue shops, at specialty kitchenware stores, or through online sources, and long-handled wooden paddles, spoons, or grill spatulas. The perforations in the grill wok allow for more of the wood and charcoal aromas to penetrate the foods in the wok. Lightly coat the inside and outside of the grill wok with cooking oil. The recipes in this book usually call for you to marinate the food to be stir-grilled first, so after you've done that, place the prepared wok in the sink and then place the marinated food

- Ketchup

- Maple syrup

- Mayonnaise

- Mustard, including grainy and Dijon style

- Oil: extra virgin olive, regular olive, toasted sesame, vegetable

- Olives, including Kalamata, Niçoise, and oil-cured

- Pepper: chipotle, lemon, and seasoned

- Pickles of all kinds

- Salt: celery, garlic, hickory, kosher, and sea

- Soy sauce (low sodium)

- Sun-dried tomatoes in olive oil

- Vinegar: balsamic, cider, red and white wine, rice

in the wok. The marinade or extra liquid will drain away. Place the wok on a baking sheet and take it outside to the grill. Set the wok over direct heat and, using those long-handled utensils, toss the food several times while stir-grilling.

For that tiara touch, when choosing what to stir-grill, think like a BBQ Queen. Use fresh and vividly colored vegetables cut into interesting sizes and shapes. The finished dish will have great eye appeal and will also be healthy and delicious.

Garden Grilling

You won't have to remind anyone—including yourself—to eat up the vegetables if you cook them on the grill. The good news for busy weeknights is that veggies cook quickly, taste fresh, and need a minimum of flavor accoutrements when they're grilled.

Sometimes, a richly flavored vegetable such as portobello mushrooms can take the place of meat, chicken, or fish in your meals (see page 20). Other times, a robust dish such as Stir-Grilled Root Vegetables with Asiago Polenta (page 36) gives you the bold, dominant flavor that meat dishes usually provide. Even if you're not a vegetarian, it certainly doesn't hurt to have a meal or two during the week in which the focus is primarily on fresh vegetables done to a turn on the grill.

To grill vegetables, there are just a few techniques you should know about. First, brush them with olive oil to keep them from sticking to the grill grates. Use a perforated grill rack if you're worried that a vegetable such as asparagus could fall through the grates. Second, par-cook winter squash, potatoes, and other dense vegetables first, so that they just finish on the grill. By par-cooking, you speed up the cooking time and

Grilled Garden "Sandwiches" with Smoked Mozzarella and Fresh Tomatoes 18

Sizzling Stir-Grilled Mushrooms on Grilled Bread with Herbal Vinaigrette 20

Grilled Vegetable Skewers with Parmesan Herb Baste 22

Blistered Whole Squash, Peppers, and Scallions with Goat Cheese 24

Grilled Vegetable Roll-Ups with Feta-Olive-Lemon Filling 26

Grilled Tofu and Japanese Vegetables with Ponzu Sauce 28

Grilled Portobello "Pizzas" 30

Grilled Pita Bread with Grilled Baba Ghanoush and Fresh Cucumber 32

Grilled Bread Sticks, Asparagus, and Carrots with Camembert Fonduta 34

Stir-Grilled Root Vegetables with Asiago Polenta 36

Grilled Polenta with Smoky Mushroom Cream Sauce 38

Grilled Polenta with Herb Cheese and Stir-Grilled Garlic Greens 40

avoid getting too much char on the vegetables. Third, use your perforated grill wok to stir-grill smaller vegetables such as cherry tomatoes and small pieces of vegetables for a fast and easy dish. And fourth, grill extra veggies to have on hand for sandwiches or salads during the rest of the week.

To make the most of your vegetables, why not grill them on skewers? From your basic bamboo, soaked first in water for 30 minutes prior to grilling, to all kinds of fancier options, vegetables look great on a skewer. At our local Whole Foods Market, we can find long fresh rosemary branches that make great skewers for vegetables. Likewise, branches of lemongrass, spikes of fresh sugar cane, or even your basic backyard campfire stick can add interest to the plate.

Grilled Garden "Sandwiches" with Smoked Mozzarella and Fresh Tomatoes

No one will ask "Where's the beef?" when you serve these fresh-from-the-grill sandwiches, a boon for those watching their carbohydrates. Instead of bread, slices of grilled zucchini, eggplant, and yellow summer squash enclose a melting smoked cheese such as mozzarella or gouda. Add the fresh tang of tomatoes and an aromatic hit from basil, and you've got a delicious one-dish vegetarian meal.

SERVES 4

I large eggplant, ends trimmed and cut lengthwise into ¹/₂-inch-thick slices

I medium-size zucchini, ends trimmed and cut lengthwise into ¹/₂-inch-thick slices

I medium-size yellow summer squash, ends trimmed and cut lengthwise into ¹/₂-inch-thick slices

Olive oil for brushing

2 large beefsteak tomatoes, chopped

¹/₂ cup chopped fresh basil

2 tablespoons olive oil

Fine kosher or sea salt and freshly ground black pepper to taste

I pound smoked mozzarella or gouda cheese, thinly sliced

You've Got Dinner!
LEMON RICE (PAGE 156)

1 Prepare a hot fire in your grill.

2 Brush both sides of the vegetable slices with olive oil and place on a baking sheet with the sliced cheese to take out to the grill. In a bowl, combine the chopped tomatoes with the basil and olive oil, and season with salt and pepper. Set aside.

3 Grill the vegetable slices for 3 to 5 minutes on one side, or until they get good grill marks, then turn. Place a layer of cheese on the cooked side of half of the eggplant, zucchini, and yellow squash slices. Top each with another vegetable slice, cooked side down. Grill for 2 to 3 minutes, pressing down

with the grill spatula, then turn and finish grilling. The vegetable slices should have good grill marks and be softened, and the cheese filling should be melted. Transfer back to the baking sheet to bring to the table.

4 Serve the sandwiches topped with the chopped tomato and fresh basil mixture.

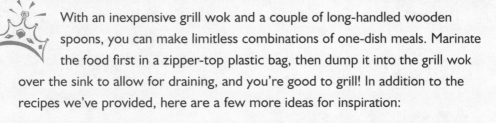

LIFE IN THE FAST LANE: STIR-GRILLING COMBOS

With an inexpensive grill wok and a couple of long-handled wooden spoons, you can make limitless combinations of one-dish meals. Marinate the food first in a zipper-top plastic bag, then dump it into the grill wok over the sink to allow for draining, and you're good to grill! In addition to the recipes we've provided, here are a few more ideas for inspiration:

- Beef strips with Orange and Red Onion Mojo (page 108), cherry tomatoes, coarsely chopped red onion, and cubed zucchini

- Cubed pork tenderloin with store-bought chipotle vinaigrette or marinade, chopped red pepper, cubed yellow squash, and slivered onion

- Cubed chicken and broccolini stalks with Hoisin Barbecue Marinade (page 156)

- Cubed chicken with store-bought Caesar dressing, black olives, mushrooms, and slivered sweet onion

- Shrimp with Orange-Coconut Dressing (page 58), mandarin orange segments, and 1-inch chunks of hearts of palm

- Italian sausage, cut into 1-inch pieces, with bell pepper strips (red, yellow, and green), cremini mushrooms, and coarsely chopped red onion

Sizzling Stir-Grilled Mushrooms on Grilled Bread with Herbal Vinaigrette

Mushrooms this good are easily a meatless meal even for the staunchest of carnivores. The mushrooms must be very fresh, especially the morels, which can fall apart quickly when tossed in the grill wok. The white and porcini mushrooms are best with closed caps, and make sure the gills on the oyster and portobello mushrooms are firm. Choose your favorite artisan bread, perhaps flavored with Parmesan, chile, sesame semolina, rosemary and olive, etc. If you prefer, you can toast the bread in a toaster or your oven. Pour a glass of crisp, dry white wine. Dine *al fresco*. Heaven!

SERVES 4

Herbal Vinaigrette
MAKES ABOUT 1 CUP

$^{1}/_{4}$ **cup dry white wine**

$^{1}/_{2}$ **cup extra virgin olive oil**

1 tablespoon balsamic vinegar

4 cloves garlic, minced

1 tablespoon chopped fresh parsley

1 tablespoon snipped chives

1 teaspoon chopped fresh rosemary

1 teaspoon chopped fresh sage

1 teaspoon chopped fresh thyme

Kosher or sea salt and freshly ground black pepper to taste

$^{1}/_{4}$ **pound morel mushrooms**

$^{1}/_{4}$ **pound white mushrooms**

$^{1}/_{4}$ **pound oyster mushrooms**

$^{1}/_{4}$ **pound shiitake mushrooms, stems removed and sliced**

$^{1}/_{4}$ **pound portobello mushrooms, sliced**

$^{1}/_{4}$ **pound porcini mushrooms**

$^1/_4$ **cup olive oil**

Kosher or sea salt and freshly ground black pepper to taste

8 slices crusty artisan bread

4 garden-grown tomatoes, sliced

I red onion, thinly sliced

I cup pitted oil-cured olives

1   Prepare a hot fire in your grill. Lightly oil a large grill wok on both sides and set on the hot grill.

2   Combine all the *Herbal Vinaigrette* ingredients in a large glass jar. Close the lid and shake vigorously. Set aside.

3   Place all the mushrooms in a large bowl. Drizzle the olive oil over the mushrooms and lightly toss to coat. Season with salt and pepper. Place the bowl on a baking sheet to take out to the grill, along with the bread slices.

4   At the grill, place the bread on the grill for 1 to 2 minutes per side, until a light golden brown. Remove and set aside. Place the mushrooms in the grill wok and close the grill lid. Cook for about 3 minutes, open the grill and toss the mushrooms with wooden spoons, and close the grill again. Repeat until the mushrooms are tender, about 10 minutes.

5   Place 1 piece of bread on each plate and cover with mushrooms. Keep 1 piece of bread on the side. Serve a sliced tomato with sliced red onion and olives to the side of the mushrooms. Drizzle all with the reserved vinaigrette and serve.

TIME-SAVING TIARA TOUCH

Good-quality artisan bread, made without preservatives, actually stays moist and fresh longer than regular bakery bread. Keep a loaf in your freezer as a "frozen asset."

Grilled Vegetable Skewers with Parmesan Herb Baste

When you use fresh rosemary branches as skewers, all of a sudden you've got a chic new way to eat kabobs. The Parmesan Herb Baste is so delicious and simple to prepare. Try it on grilled chicken, tossed with cooked mushrooms, and as a bread spread. You can also serve these skewers with pasta tossed simply with olive oil, minced garlic, salt, and pepper.

SERVES 4

Parmesan Herb Baste

MAKES ABOUT $^1/_2$ CUP

1/2 tablespoon dried basil

I teaspoon freshly ground black pepper

1/4 cup freshly grated Parmesan cheese

4 tablespoons olive oil

2 tablespoons red wine vinegar

16 fresh rosemary branches (or 8 wooden skewers, soaked in water for at least 30 minutes prior to grilling)

I pint cherry tomatoes

2 small yellow summer squash, ends trimmed and cut into I-inch pieces

2 small zucchini, ends trimmed and cut into I-inch pieces

8 ounces whole white mushrooms

I large red onion, peeled and cut into 8 wedges

Extra virgin olive oil for drizzling

Freshly grated Parmesan cheese for garnish

You've Got Dinner!

GRILLED GARLIC BREAD STUFFED WITH FONTINA CHEESE

FRESH FRUIT SALAD

1   In a small bowl, mix the *Parmesan Herb Baste* ingredients together.

2   Prepare a hot fire in your grill.

3   With your fingers, remove all but the top 2 inches of rosemary needles on each branch, reserving the needles for another use. Starting at the bare end of each branch, thread the different vegetable pieces onto each skewer, using only 1 onion wedge per skewer. Brush each skewer with some of the herb baste and place the skewers on a baking sheet to take out to the grill, along with the remaining baste.

4   Grill each skewer for 4 to 5 minutes per side, brushing with the baste, until the vegetables have good grill marks. Serve hot, drizzled with olive oil and garnished with Parmesan.

Blistered Whole Squash, Peppers, and Scallions with Goat Cheese

When zucchini and yellow summer squash are readily available, give this dish a try. Select the smallest, firmest squash. Choose a variety of whole bell peppers to turn this platter of grilled food into a rainbow of colors. It will be as beautiful as it is delicious. For chile-heads, add a variety of hot peppers, too, such as banana, serrano, jalapeño, etc. If you're a carnivore, add the grilled meat(s) of your choice. Otherwise, get ready for a very healthy veg-out (instead of a pig-out). For company, put the vegetables on a platter and serve with a duo of dressings. We suggest Tarragon Vinaigrette (page 64) and Lemon Dressing (page 46).

SERVES 4

20 green onions

8 small zucchini

8 small yellow summer squash

6 bell peppers in assorted colors

8 assorted hot peppers, or more to your taste (optional)

3 to 4 tablespoons olive oil

Kosher or sea salt and freshly ground black pepper to taste

1 1/2 cups (12 ounces) crumbled goat cheese

You've Got Dinner!

MULTIGRAIN BREAD WITH HERB BUTTER

GREEN SALAD OR SLICED TOMATOES

1   Prepare a hot fire in your grill.

2   Place the green onions, zucchini, yellow summer squash, bell peppers, and hot peppers, if using, on a baking sheet and drizzle with the olive oil, turning to coat everything lightly. Season with salt and pepper.

3   Place the vegetables over the hot fire and grill, turning them several times until they are charred on the outside and cooked through to your liking, 15 to 20 minutes.

4   Place the vegetables on a platter and sprinkle with the crumbled goat cheese. For a spectacular presentation, arrange a row of the green onions, then a row of the green charred zucchini, followed by the yellow summer squash and the peppers. Serve hot or at room temperature.

LIFE IN THE FAST LANE: DRIZZLES

One bottle, three uses. Take that bottle of Italian vinaigrette and make it your blank canvas for a quick marinade, a handy baste, or a finishing drizzle. Then drizzle (or marinate) fish, shellfish, chicken, turkey, vegetables, game, beef, and pork. Here are four versatile variations for a special finishing touch:

Asia Meets Italy Drizzle: Pour 1 cup Italian vinaigrette into a 2-cup glass jar with a tight-fitting lid. Add $1/4$ cup soy sauce and 2 teaspoons toasted sesame oil. Shake to blend.

Citrus Herb Drizzle: Pour 1 cup Italian vinaigrette into a 2-cup glass jar with a tight-fitting lid. Add the zest and juice of an orange, lemon, or lime to taste. Add 2 teaspoons dried *herbes de Provence*, or fresh chopped herbs to taste (about 2 tablespoons). Shake to blend.

Greek Island Drizzle: Pour 1 cup Italian vinaigrette into a 2-cup glass jar with a tight-fitting lid. Add $1/4$ cup crumbled feta cheese and $1/4$ cup pitted and chopped Kalamata olives. Shake to blend.

Hold On to Your Hat Drizzle: Pour 1 cup Italian vinaigrette into a 2-cup glass jar with a tight-fitting lid. Add $1/4$ cup bottled chipotle sauce and 2 tablespoons chopped fresh cilantro. Shake to blend.

Grilled Vegetable Roll-Ups with Feta-Olive-Lemon Filling

In the back of your mind, you can still hear your mother saying, "Eat your vegetables," can't you? With this recipe for a vegetarian feast, you won't need to be reminded. Before you go out to the grill, make the filling. If you like, add a dipping sauce of your favorite garlicky vinaigrette. All you need with this is a loaf of good, crusty bread. Yum!

SERVES 4

Feta-Olive-Lemon Filling

 I cup (8 ounces) crumbled feta cheese

 I tablespoon olive oil

 I clove garlic, minced

 $1/2$ cup finely chopped Kalamata or Niçoise olives

 2 tablespoons finely chopped green onions (white part with some of the green)

 I teaspoon grated lemon zest

 I large Japanese eggplant, ends trimmed and cut lengthwise into $1/2$-inch-thick strips

 I medium-size zucchini, ends trimmed and cut lengthwise into $1/2$-inch-thick strips

 I medium-size yellow summer squash, ends trimmed and cut lengthwise into $1/2$-inch-thick strips

 Olive oil for brushing

 Fine kosher or sea salt and freshly ground black pepper to taste

1 Prepare a hot fire in your grill.

2 Combine the *Feta-Olive-Lemon Filling* ingredients in a bowl until well blended. Set aside. Brush the eggplant, zucchini, and yellow summer

squash slices with olive oil and season with salt and pepper. Place on a baking sheet to take out to the grill.

3   Grill the vegetable slices for 3 to 4 minutes on each side, or until both sides have good grill marks and the vegetables are softened. Transfer to the tray and bring back inside.

4   While the vegetable slices are still warm from the grill, place about 1 tablespoon of the feta filling on the end third of each slice and roll up. If necessary, secure each roll-up with a toothpick. Arrange the roll-ups on a platter. Serve warm or at room temperature.

Grilled Tofu and Japanese Vegetables with Ponzu Sauce

We have to admit that normally we're not the biggest tofu fans, but it's a food with a lot going for it and it's delicious served this way. Tofu is high in protein, is low in fat, and has an ancient lineage in the Far East. It's usually available in two forms: silken and firm. For grilling, you want firm. And, actually, some of the best artisan-made tofu comes from Lawrence, Kansas, about 30 minutes from where Judith lives. Tofu in Kansas? Well, why not, since soybeans are a major U.S. crop? One of the earliest ways of cooking tofu was over an open fire—a recipe known in Japan as *yaki-dofu*, or "grilled tofu," so everything old is new again here. We like to add grilled Japanese eggplant and baby bok choy to the fire, then serve everything with the tangy Ponzu Sauce, either for dipping or for drizzling. It's a great marinade for poultry, pork, and fish, too.

SERVES 4

Ponzu Sauce
MAKES ABOUT 1 CUP

4 tablespoons soy sauce or tamari

2 tablespoons rice vinegar

1 1/2 tablespoons raw, turbinado, or light brown sugar

1 tablespoon fresh lemon juice

1 tablespoon fresh lime juice

1 teaspoon grated fresh ginger

2 tablespoons very finely chopped green onions (white part with some of the green)

1 pound firm tofu, cut into 1/2-inch-thick triangles

2 small Japanese eggplants, ends trimmed and cut lengthwise into 1/2-inch-thick slices

You've Got Dinner!
STEAMED RICE OR UDON NOODLES

8 whole baby bok choy or 2 large heads of bok choy cut into quarters

1 bunch green onions

1 cup store-bought teriyaki marinade of your choice

Vegetable oil for brushing

1   Whisk the *Ponzu Sauce* ingredients together in a bowl and set aside.

2   Place the tofu and vegetables in a large bowl or deep baking pan and sprinkle with the teriyaki marinade. Let sit for 15 minutes before you start the grill.

3   Prepare a hot fire in your grill.

4   Pat the tofu and vegetables dry with paper towels, place on a baking sheet, and brush with vegetable oil. Grill the tofu for 3 to 4 minutes per side, or until it gets good grill marks. Grill the vegetables for 2 to 3 minutes per side, turning once, until they have good grill marks and are softened.

5   To serve, portion the tofu and vegetables among 4 plates and serve with the ponzu sauce drizzled over the top or in dipping bowls on the side.

TIME-SAVING TIARA TOUCH

The Ponzu Sauce can be made ahead and stored for up to 1 week in the refrigerator.

Grilled Portobello "Pizzas"

The BBQ Queens love this delicious update on pizza without a crust. Make more portobellos than you need because you can easily wrap up one pizza to take to work and zap in the microwave for a hearty, healthy lunch. Pair this dish with a young red wine, such as a Chianti (not if you're at work, of course—we wouldn't want to get you into trouble).

SERVES 4

1 medium-size yellow bell pepper, cored, seeded, and cut into long strips

1 medium-size red bell pepper, cored, seeded, and cut into long strips

1 medium-size green bell pepper, cored, seeded, and cut into long strips

2 cloves garlic, minced

4 tablespoons olive oil

4 large portobello mushroom caps

Kosher or sea salt and freshly ground black pepper to taste

4 tablespoons pizza sauce

2 cups shredded mozzarella cheese

You've Got Dinner!
GRILLED GARLIC BREAD
GREEN SALAD

1 Prepare a medium-hot fire in your grill. Oil a perforated grill rack and set aside.

2 Place the pepper strips and garlic in a zipper-top plastic bag, pour in 2 tablespoons of the olive oil, seal the bag, and shake to coat. Brush the portobellos with the remaining 2 tablespoons of olive oil and season with salt and pepper. Place the bag of pepper strips and the portobellos on a baking sheet, along with the pizza sauce and cheese, and take to the grill.

3 Place the pepper strips on the prepared perforated grill rack and the portobellos directly on the grill grate. Grill, with the lid closed, for 8 to 10 minutes,

until the vegetables have softened and browned, turning once. Top each portobello with 1 tablespoon of the pizza sauce, one-fourth of the grilled peppers, and ½ cup of the grated mozzarella. Close the lid, and grill for 2 to 5 minutes more, or until the cheese has melted. Serve hot.

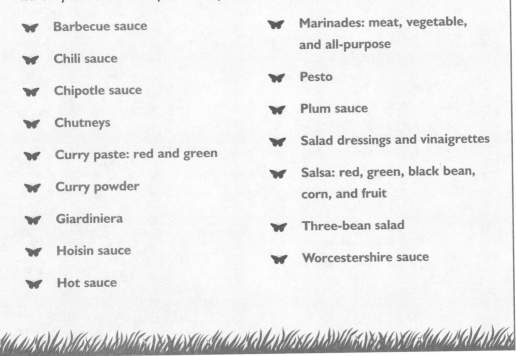

LIFE IN THE FAST LANE: MESSAGE IN A BOTTLE

Whether we save time by using a bottled dressing or get a punch of flavor with thyme in a bottle, the BBQ Queens love good-quality convenience products. Our list of must-haves includes many ethnic items we like to keep on hand. So you wouldn't necessarily have to choose everything we list here—just the kinds of pre-made products that you know you will use.

- Barbecue sauce
- Chili sauce
- Chipotle sauce
- Chutneys
- Curry paste: red and green
- Curry powder
- Giardiniera
- Hoisin sauce
- Hot sauce

- Marinades: meat, vegetable, and all-purpose
- Pesto
- Plum sauce
- Salad dressings and vinaigrettes
- Salsa: red, green, black bean, corn, and fruit
- Three-bean salad
- Worcestershire sauce

Grilled Pita Bread with Grilled Baba Ghanoush and Fresh Cucumber

When the weather is warm, or you just want to pretend it is, head out to the grill to turn a traditional Middle Eastern appetizer into your main dish. To make it easy on yourself, purchase ready-made marinated vegetables, hummus, olives, or other goodies to serve with the grilled pita bread and baba ghanoush. You're getting three vegetables here, so celebrate this easy way to eat healthfully.

SERVES 4

Grilled Baba Ghanoush

MAKES ABOUT 2 CUPS

I large eggplant, ends trimmed and cut lengthwise into 1-inch-thick slices

I large red bell pepper

2 tablespoons olive oil, plus more for brushing

$^1/_4$ cup fresh cilantro sprigs

2 cloves garlic

2 tablespoons fresh lemon juice, or more to your taste

I teaspoon ground cumin

$^1/_4$ teaspoon ground coriander

$^1/_4$ teaspoon cayenne pepper, or more to your taste

Fine kosher or sea salt to taste

8 large pita bread rounds

2 medium-size cucumbers, cut into slices

You've Got Dinner!
HOMEMADE HUMMUS (PAGE 70), IF YOU WISH

1   Prepare a hot fire in your grill.

2   To make the *Grilled Baba Ghanoush*, brush the eggplant slices and red bell pepper with olive oil and place on a baking sheet. Place the remaining baba ghanoush ingredients in the bowl of a food processor and set aside. Brush

the pita breads with olive oil on both sides and place on the baking sheet to take out to the grill.

3   Grill the eggplant slices, turning once, until you have good grill marks and the eggplant is tender, 8 to 10 minutes total. Transfer back to the baking sheet. Grill the red pepper, turning several times, until it is blackened and blistered all over, 10 to 15 minutes total. Transfer back to the baking sheet. Grill the pita breads, turning once, until they have good grill marks, about 5 minutes total. Transfer to the baking sheet, cover with foil, and keep warm.

4   Add the grilled eggplant slices to the food processor. Carefully cut the pepper in half, remove the seeds, charred skin, and stem and discard. Place the seeded and skinned pepper and 2 tablespoons olive oil in the food processor and puree everything. Taste, and add more lemon juice, salt, and cayenne pepper if desired.

5   To serve, place a portion of the baba ghanoush and some cucumber slices on each plate. With kitchen shears, cut the pita breads into wedges and place on each plate or in a basket to pass at the table.

TIME-SAVING TIARA TOUCH

Fire-roasted red peppers from a jar are already peeled and seeded. They are just as good as homemade, too.

Grilled Bread Sticks, Asparagus, and Carrots with Camembert Fonduta

Big name, easy recipe. And it's a great vegetarian entrée and fun finger food as well, since you'll be dipping grilled bread sticks and veggies into an Italian fondue. If you can find true baby carrots with their feathery tops, wonderful. If not, use zucchini or yellow summer squash cut into long wedges. Serve everything family-style from a big platter in the middle of the table, or arrange individual portions on each plate. (If wrapping the bread sticks is too much after a long day, feel free to skip that step.)

SERVES 4

Artichoke, Shallot, and Camembert Fonduta

One 15-ounce can artichoke hearts, chopped but not drained

2 large shallots, peeled and minced

1 clove garlic, minced

1 pound Camembert or Brie cheese, rind removed and chopped

1 pound asparagus, ends trimmed

1 pound baby carrots with tops or 2 medium-size zucchini or yellow summer squash, ends trimmed and cut lengthwise into wedges

1 pound frozen bread dough, thawed, rolled out, and cut into 2 x 8-inch fingers

8 large spinach, arugula, or Swiss chard leaves (optional)

Olive oil for brushing

Kosher or sea salt and freshly ground black pepper to taste

1   Prepare a medium-hot fire in your grill.

2   Stir together the *Artichoke, Shallot, and Camembert Fonduta* ingredients in a disposable aluminum pan.

3   Place the asparagus and carrots on a baking sheet. Wrap each finger of dough with a spinach leaf, if desired, and place on the baking sheet to take out to the grill. Brush the vegetables and leaf-wrapped dough with olive oil and season with salt and pepper.

4   Place the fonduta on the grill, close the lid, and cook for 3 to 4 minutes, or until the cheese is beginning to melt. Stir the mixture. Place the bread sticks on the grill, close the lid, and cook for 3 to 4 minutes. Turn the bread sticks with grill tongs and give the fonduta another stir. Close the lid and cook for 3 to 4 minutes more, or until the bread sticks are puffed and golden. Remove to the baking sheet and give the fonduta another stir. Place the vegetables on the grill and cook for 3 to 4 minutes, turn with grill tongs, and stir the fonduta again. Finish grilling the vegetables until slightly charred and crisp-tender.

5   To serve, transfer the fonduta to a large serving bowl or small serving bowls and place in the center of a platter or a plate. Arrange the vegetables and bread sticks around the fonduta. Dip the veggies and bread sticks into the fonduta and enjoy!

Stir-Grilled Root Vegetables with Asiago Polenta

By micro-cooking the root vegetables until almost done, you can grill these veggies in no time at all, leaving you plenty of time for a pre-dinner martini. Maybe you'll even consider this dish for the Thanksgiving table. If you make a double batch of the polenta, following our mantra of "the value of leftovers," you can spoon the extra into a loaf pan, cover, and refrigerate it for up to 3 days. Then use it to make Grilled Polenta with Smoky Mushroom Cream Sauce (page 38). It's also a wonderful side for many of the grilled meats you'll find in later chapters. If you can't find polenta, you can substitute corn grits; most grocery stores carry the Bob's Red Mill brand.

SERVES 4

Asiago Polenta
MAKES ABOUT 6 CUPS

6 cups vegetable or chicken broth

8 ounces uncooked polenta (stone-ground Italian yellow cornmeal) or corn grits

1 cup freshly grated Asiago cheese

Fine kosher or sea salt and freshly ground black pepper to taste

8 shallots, peeled

8 baby turnips, peeled, or 4 medium-size turnips, peeled and quartered

4 baby carrots

8 new potatoes, quartered

1 large leek, trimmed to about a 5-inch length, sliced in half lengthwise, and chopped

1 large parsnip, peeled and cut into 2-inch pieces

3 tablespoons olive oil

Kosher or sea salt and freshly ground white pepper to taste

1   To make the *Asiago Polenta*, in a large pot over medium-high heat, bring the broth to a boil. Sprinkle in the polenta in a steady stream, whisking constantly. Continue whisking for 5 minutes. When the polenta has bubbled into a thick mass, whisk in the Asiago cheese. Season with salt and black pepper and set aside, keeping warm.

2   Prepare a hot fire in your grill.

3   Place all the vegetables in a large, microwave-safe bowl, toss with the olive oil, and season with salt and white pepper. Microwave on high for 3 to 4 minutes, or until the vegetables are partially cooked. Pour the vegetables into a grill wok and place the wok on a baking sheet to take out to the grill.

4   Stir-grill the vegetables, tossing with wooden paddles or grill spatulas, until the potatoes, parsnips, and turnips are tender when pierced with a paring knife. Serve them next to or on top of the warm polenta.

Grilled Polenta with Smoky Mushroom Cream Sauce

This is a wonderful dish to serve in spring or fall, when mushrooms are at their peak. You can use a blend of wild and domestic mushrooms, if you like. We've added dried porcinis for extra depth of flavor. By making the sauce on the grill, you get a smokier result than you would indoors, which adds to the flavor. If you have made extra Asiago Polenta (from Stir-Grilled Root Vegetables with Asiago Polenta on page 36), you can use it in this recipe. Spoon it into a loaf pan and let it chill overnight in the refrigerator. When you're ready to grill, cut it into ¹/₂-inch-thick slices to make this dish. If you don't have any leftover polenta, just use the ready-made store-bought polenta sold in tubes and sprinkle it with cheese, as we do here.

SERVES 4

Smoky Mushroom Cream Sauce

MAKES ABOUT 2 CUPS

¹/₄ **cup dried porcini mushrooms, sliced, or other dried mushrooms**

¹/₂ **cup boiling water**

2 tablespoons unsalted butter

8 ounces sliced fresh assorted mushrooms of your choice (about 2 cups)

1¹/₂ **cups heavy cream**

1 tablespoon Dijon mustard

1 tablespoon brandy, whiskey, or Scotch (optional)

Fine kosher or sea salt and freshly ground black pepper to taste

One 16-ounce package store-bought prepared polenta, cut into ¹/₂**-inch-thick slices**

Olive oil for brushing

1 cup freshly grated Asiago cheese

You've Got Dinner!

GREEN SALAD

FRESH FRUIT SALAD

1 To start the *Smoky Mushroom Cream Sauce*, place the dried porcini mushrooms in a small bowl and pour the boiling water over them. Let sit for 10 minutes, or until softened. Place the bowl on a baking sheet.

2 Prepare a medium-hot fire in your grill.

3 Place the butter and fresh mushrooms in a disposable aluminum pan and place on the baking sheet to take out to the grill. Mix the cream, mustard, and brandy, if using, in a small bowl and also place on the baking sheet. Set aside.

4 Brush the polenta slices with olive oil and place on a second baking sheet. Put the cheese in a small bowl and put that on the baking sheet. Take both sheets out to the grill.

5 Place the pan of butter and mushrooms over direct heat and stir with grill tongs until the mushrooms sizzle and begin to give up their juices, 4 to 5 minutes. Stir in the porcini mixture and the cream mixture and cook, stirring every minute or so, until the cream comes to a boil. Transfer the sauce to a cooler spot on the grill, season with salt and pepper, and let simmer while you grill the polenta.

6 Place the polenta slices on the grill grates and grill for 2 to 3 minutes per side, or until you get good grill marks. Turn once and top each slice with a sprinkling of cheese. Arrange the polenta slices on 4 plates and top with the sauce. Serve hot.

Grilled Polenta with Herb Cheese and Stir-Grilled Garlic Greens

This super-easy entrée could make flexitarians (people who eat both vegetarian and meat/fish/poultry diets) out of the most die-hard meat eaters. It's robust, colorful, and healthy. (But don't let that put you off!)

SERVES 4

One 16-ounce package store-bought prepared polenta, cut into $1/2$-inch-thick slices

Olive oil for brushing

3 tablespoons olive oil

3 garlic cloves, minced

$1/4$ teaspoon red pepper flakes

1 pound Swiss chard or kale, tough stems removed and torn into small pieces

1 pound baby spinach

Fine kosher or sea salt and freshly ground black pepper to taste

One 7-ounce package herbed cream cheese, such as Boursin

You've Got Dinner!
A PLATTER OF THICKLY SLICED FRESH TOMATOES

1 Prepare a medium-hot fire in your grill.

2 Brush the polenta slices with olive oil and place on a baking sheet. In a small bowl, combine the olive oil, garlic, and red pepper flakes. Place the Swiss chard and spinach in a large bowl and drizzle the olive oil mixture over the greens. Toss to coat, then season with salt and pepper. Place the greens in a perforated grill wok and put the wok on the sheet with the polenta. Take everything out to the grill.

3 Place the grill wok on the grill grates and toss the greens with wooden paddles or grill spatulas until they are wilted and slightly browned. Remove from the grill and set aside. Place the polenta slices on the grill grates and grill for 2 to 3 minutes per side, or until you get good grill marks.

4   Spread the herbed cheese over each grilled polenta slice, arrange the slices on 4 plates, and top with the wilted greens. Serve warm or at room temperature.

LIFE IN THE FAST LANE: DÉJÀ VU DINNERS

The BBQ Queens decree: grill once, eat twice! We ascribe to the philosophy of the value of leftovers. Maximize your time at the grill and cook extra food while you polish off that glass of wine. After all, grilled leftovers aren't like other leftovers. They taste better! Put those leftovers or extra grilled foods to good use in salads, sandwiches, or soups for another meal during the week, or even a delicious lunch to take to work. And don't forget that leftover grilled hamburgers and turkey burgers can be refrigerated and then quickly microwaved, and they will retain all of their smoky juiciness.

We've given you lots of ideas throughout this book for creative ways to make your investment of time at the grill pay big dividends. Some of the recipes that can be made in a flash by using leftovers are Grilled Pork Tenderloin Salad with Toasted Pecan Vinaigrette (page 52); Tropical Chicken and Rice Salad with Orange-Coconut Dressing (page 58); Grilled Steak Sandwiches with Aioli, Tomatoes, and Arugula (page 74); Wood-Grilled Shrimp Quesadillas (page 226); Grilled Chicken Pasta with Tomatoes, Fresh Thyme, and Brine-Cured Olives (page 160); and Grilled Polenta with Smoky Mushroom Cream Sauce (page 38).

Salad du Jour

Sometimes the BBQ Queens just crave a good salad. (Maybe it's the estrogen.) There's no better canvas for fresh flavors than a big bowl of leafy greens. A main-course salad shows off all the best seasonal and regional ingredients, with a hint of sizzle and smoke from something grilled and a drizzle of dressing. There, aren't you craving a salad now?

Whether you head out to the grill first with the intention of creating a salad or you make up the salad and then add foods you've previously grilled, you'll get a dish that's colorful and creative. Add a flavorful, but not overpowering, dressing and you've got a meal in a bowl with a surprise in every bite.

Remember, grill once, eat twice! So get out there and improvise! Cruise your favorite grocery store or farmers' market for the freshest baby greens, the coolest cucumbers, the tangiest tomatoes. Stock your pantry with canned beans and black-eyed peas, mandarin oranges, hearts of palm, and artichoke hearts. Pick fresh herb leaves from your garden or from potted plants on your windowsill. Toss in those luscious grilled shrimp, that oh-so-good steak, or that yummy chicken or pork

Grilled Chopped Vegetable Salad with Tomatoes, Feta, and Olives 44

Lebanese Grilled Flatbread Salad with Grilled Haloumi Cheese 46

Stir-Grilled Asian Beef Salad with Fresh Mint 48

Grilled Pork Tenderloin Salad with Steamed Baby New Potatoes and Anchovy Caper Vinaigrette 50

Grilled Pork Tenderloin Salad with Toasted Pecan Vinaigrette 52

Mesquite-Grilled Pasta Salad with Chicken, Peaches, and Cashews 54

Stir-Grilled Chicken Salad with Asparagus and Blue Cheese 56

Tropical Chicken and Rice Salad with Orange-Coconut Dressing 58

Grilled Turkey Tenderloin Salad with Green Curry Dressing 60

Low Country Black-Eyed Pea and Grilled Jumbo Shrimp Salad with Hot Bacon Dressing 62

Grilled Scallop and Heart of Palm Salad with Tarragon Vinaigrette 64

tenderloin. Top with crumbled mellow or assertive cheeses, from goat to blue. And always have fresh garlic, good olive oil, and fresh lemons on hand for a simply satisfying vinaigrette to whisk together at the last minute.

Give in to that impulse. Be the star chef with your own salad du jour.

Grilled Chopped Vegetable Salad with Tomatoes, Feta, and Olives

Keep it simple here. Go to your garden or the farmers' market and pick some fresh vegetables, slice them and brush with olive oil, grill them quickly, then chop and dress for a deliciously easy salad with rib-sticking appeal. We love this drizzled with our favorite dressing, our friend Mary Pfeifer's Work of Art Vinaigrette, which you make with a mortar and pestle in seconds. This small amount of vinaigrette can easily—and surprisingly—dress a large bowl of salad. Instead of feta, try crumbles of blue cheese, *queso fresco*, or goat cheese. With a loaf of crusty bread warmed on the grill, you've got a simple yet sophisticated meal.

SERVES 4

Work of Art Vinaigrette
MAKES ABOUT $1/4$ CUP

1 large clove garlic

1 teaspoon coarse kosher or sea salt

3 tablespoons extra virgin olive oil

1 tablespoon fresh lemon juice

4 small zucchini, ends trimmed and cut lengthwise into 1/2-inch-thick slices

4 small yellow summer squash, ends trimmed and cut lengthwise into $1/2$-inch-thick slices

1 large eggplant, ends trimmed and cut lengthwise into $1/2$-inch-thick slices

1 medium-size red bell pepper

15 green onions, ends trimmed

Olive oil for brushing

Fine kosher or sea salt and freshly ground black pepper to taste

1 cup cherry or grape tomatoes, halved

1 cup brine-cured Kalamata or Niçoise olives, pitted

$^1/_2$ cup (4 ounces) crumbled feta cheese

1   To make the *Work of Art Vinaigrette*, place the garlic and salt in a mortar and crush with the pestle. Keep crushing in a circular motion until the garlic is pureed. Stir in the olive oil and lemon juice with the pestle and taste for seasoning. Set aside.

2   Prepare a hot fire in your grill.

3   Brush the vegetable slices, whole red bell pepper, and green onions with olive oil, season with salt and pepper, and place on a baking sheet to take out to the grill.

4   Grill the slices, turning once, for 3 to 4 minutes per side, or until you have good grill marks. Grill the bell pepper, turning several times, until the skin is charred and blistered all over. Place the green onions perpendicular to the grill grates (so they don't fall through) and grill until you have good grill marks, about 2 minutes per side. Transfer everything to the baking sheet.

5   Chop the grilled vegetable slices and green onions into bite-size pieces. Let the red pepper cool slightly, then remove the skin, seeds, and stem with a paring knife and discard; chop the red pepper flesh. Combine the chopped vegetables with the tomatoes and olives in a large serving bowl. Toss with the vinaigrette and top with crumbled feta. Serve family-style.

TIME-SAVING TIARA TOUCH

Make a little extra grilled vegetables to toss with pasta for dinner tomorrow.

Lebanese Grilled Flatbread Salad with Grilled Haloumi Cheese

Known as "fattoush," this salad is a cousin of the Tuscan panzanella, both of which are made with bread. You'll want to use kitchen shears or a paring knife to help separate each pita into two thin rounds. Brush them with olive oil, then grill until crispy. The contrast of crisp and slightly smoky bread and cheese with fresh salad ingredients is very refreshing. This salad is vegetarian in spirit, but add grilled shrimp, chicken, or beef if you like. Haloumi cheese is a sheep's milk cheese that takes to the grill very well. If you can't find haloumi, use a wheel of baby Brie. Sumac is a dried red Middle Eastern seasoning (made from the berries of a sumac tree) with a sharp, sour taste. It adds a distinctive flavor, so sprinkle it on! Pass more pita bread at the table, if you wish.

SERVES 4

Lemon Dressing
MAKES ABOUT I CUP

- 1 clove garlic, minced
- 5 tablespoons fresh lemon juice
- 3 tablespoons extra virgin olive oil
- Fine kosher or sea salt and freshly ground black pepper to taste

- 4 large pita bread rounds, separated into 8 thin rounds
- 16 ounces haloumi cheese, cut into $^1/_2$-inch-thick slices, or a wheel of baby Brie
- Olive oil for brushing
- One 8-ounce bag mixed lettuces
- 2 medium-size tomatoes, diced
- 4 green onions, finely chopped (white and green parts)
- $^1/_4$ cup chopped fresh mint

¹/₄ cup chopped fresh cilantro

¹/₄ cup chopped fresh Italian parsley

Ground sumac for sprinkling

1   To make the *Lemon Dressing*, whisk the garlic, lemon juice, and olive oil in a small bowl. Season with salt and pepper and set aside.

2   Prepare a medium-hot fire in your grill. Oil a perforated grill rack.

3   Brush the pita rounds and haloumi cheese on both sides with the olive oil. Use kitchen shears to cut each round of bread into triangles. Place on a baking sheet and take out to the grill.

4   Place the pita triangles on the prepared grill rack. Grill the pita pieces, turning once, for 1 to 2 minutes per side, or until browned and crisp. Grill the haloumi on the prepared grill rack for 1 to 2 minutes per side (the baby Brie for 3 to 4 minutes per side), or until the cheese has softened but not melted and you have good grill marks.

5   Combine the grilled pita triangles with the lettuce, tomatoes, green onions, and herbs in a large bowl. Pour the dressing over the salad and toss well. Portion the salad onto 4 plates, with slices of grilled haloumi alongside. Sprinkle sumac over all and serve.

Stir-Grilled Asian Beef Salad with Fresh Mint

The mint in this recipe is used as a salad green for a refreshingly flavorful salad. So grow your own (and watch it take over that barren patch in your garden) or buy it at a farmers' market. You can also just substitute the salad greens of your choice. If you like, grill a few flatbreads brushed with oil when you stir-grill the beef. You can also use the marinade for fish, poultry, or pork.

SERVES 4

Soy and Sesame Marinade
MAKES ABOUT I CUP

> $^1/_2$ cup low-sodium soy sauce
>
> $^1/_4$ cup sugar
>
> 3 tablespoons toasted sesame oil
>
> $^1/_2$ teaspoon freshly ground black pepper
>
> 4 green onions, chopped (white and green parts)
>
> 3 cloves garlic, minced
>
> I jalapeño pepper, seeded and chopped
>
> I tablespoon vegetable oil
>
> I to I$^1/_2$ pounds lean boneless beef steak (sirloin, round, or chuck), sliced into thin strips
>
> I cup fresh mint leaves
>
> 3 cups fresh salad greens (assorted lettuces of your choice)
>
> Toasted sesame seeds for garnish

You've Got Dinner!
STEAMED RICE AS A BED FOR THE SALAD

I   In a small bowl, whisk the *Soy and Sesame Marinade* ingredients together. Place the beef in a zipper-top plastic bag, pour half the marinade over the beef, seal the bag, and toss to blend. Set aside to marinate for 15 minutes. Reserve the remaining marinade.

2   Prepare a hot fire in your grill.

3   Arrange the mint leaves and lettuces on 4 plates. Place a grill wok in your sink, pour the contents of the zipper-top bag into the wok, and let drain. Place the wok on a doubled baking sheet and take out to the grill.

4   Stir-grill the beef, using wooden paddles or grill spatulas, until cooked to medium, about 15 minutes. Place the wok on the clean baking sheet and bring inside. To serve, place the stir-grilled beef on top of the greens and drizzle with the reserved marinade. Sprinkle with the sesame seeds.

LIFE IN THE FAST LANE: MICROWAVE TIPS

1   *Toast nuts, bread crumbs, and coconut—fast!* Spread them out on a microwave-safe plate in a single layer. Heat on high for 2 to 3 minutes, stirring every minute. Note that they will continue to toast for about a minute after removal.

2   *Get more juice from citrus fruits.* A refrigerated lemon or lime is more difficult to juice than one that is at room temperature or slightly warm. To get the most juice, microwave citrus fruits for 20 seconds before squeezing.

3   *Cook vegetables quickly.* All vegetables can be steamed in the microwave without adding water. Place them in one layer (if possible) on a dish, cover with a paper towel, and cook on high. The timing will vary according to your microwave, but check tender items, such as spinach, mushrooms, and snow peas, after 30 seconds, and crunchy ones, including carrots, after 4 minutes. For potatoes, prick baking or sweet potatoes all over with a fork or paring knife, then micro-bake for 7 to 8 minutes, or until softened.

4   *Par-cook vegetables you want to finish on the grill.* Cut squash into rings and par-cook on high for several minutes. Prick new potatoes all over with a fork or paring knife and par-cook on high for 7 minutes.

Grilled Pork Tenderloin Salad with Steamed Baby New Potatoes and Anchovy Caper Vinaigrette

The next time you're grilling pork tenderloin, grill twice as much so that you can make this satisfying salad for a brilliant "leftover" dinner later in the week. You won't even have to fire up the grill for it. Grilled pork tenderloin can also be frozen and then thawed for this salad. Make sure you wrap it in plastic wrap, then tightly in aluminum foil, and place in a zipper-top plastic freezer bag. The key to all of this is dating the package and using the pork within 2 or 3 weeks for optimum results. The steamed red potatoes add color to the dish and make it more substantial. Choose the smallest red potatoes you can find. Then you only have to cut them in half and they will cook quickly, too.

SERVES 4

1 pound baby red potatoes

2 heads (about 1 pound) romaine lettuce

2 grilled pork tenderloins (about 1 ½ pounds)

Anchovy Caper Vinaigrette
MAKES ABOUT 1 CUP

2 tablespoons anchovy paste

2 tablespoons Dijon mustard

2 cloves garlic, minced

¼ cup balsamic vinegar

½ cup extra virgin olive oil

2 tablespoons capers

Kosher or sea salt and freshly ground black pepper to taste

You've Got Dinner!
STEAMED GREEN BEANS
OR QUICK PEPERONATA
(PAGE 168)

1 Place the potatoes in a pot and just cover with water. Place over high heat and bring to a boil. Cook until fork tender, 18 to 20 minutes. Drain into a colander and set aside.

2 Slice the romaine into $\frac{1}{2}$-inch slices and place in a large salad bowl. Slice the meat into $\frac{1}{4}$-inch-thick slices and set aside.

3 To make the *Anchovy Caper Vinaigrette*, whisk the anchovy paste, mustard, garlic, and vinegar in a medium-size bowl. Slowly add the olive oil, whisking constantly to emulsify. Stir in the capers and season with salt and pepper.

4 Add the potatoes to the lettuce. Dress with about $\frac{1}{4}$ cup of vinaigrette and toss to coat lightly. Portion the lettuce and potatoes onto each of 4 plates. Arrange the tenderloin slices on top in a fan pattern. Serve with extra vinaigrette on the side.

TIME-SAVING TIARA TOUCH

The Anchovy Caper Vinaigrette can be made ahead and stored for 1 day in the refrigerator. It's also great on green salads or a chopped tomato-and-celery salad. In a pinch, just whisk anchovy paste into store-bought Dijon vinaigrette.

Grilled Pork Tenderloin Salad with Toasted Pecan Vinaigrette

Let's hear it for fabulous vinaigrettes. Not only are they great to dress a salad and transform leftovers, as they do here, but they also can be used as dipping sauces, marinades, and bread spreads to make awesome sandwiches. The key to this dressing is toasting the pecans. Do this by placing pecans on a baking sheet and toasting in a 350°F oven for 7 to 10 minutes, or until they begin to turn a deep dark brown. Serve this salad with warm crusty bread.

SERVES 4

2 grilled pork tenderloins (about 1 1/2 pounds)

1 head leafy red lettuce, torn into bite-size pieces

2 ears grilled corn, kernels cut off (about 1 cup)

1 cup grape, cherry, or yellow pear tomatoes

1/2 cup toasted pecan halves

Toasted Pecan Vinaigrette

MAKES ABOUT 2 CUPS

1 teaspoon lemon zest

2 tablespoons fresh lemon juice

2 tablespoons tarragon vinegar

1 tablespoon Dijon mustard

1 tablespoon honey

1/4 cup toasted pecan halves

1 cup vegetable oil

Kosher or sea salt and freshly ground black pepper to taste

1 Slice the pork into 1/2-inch-thick slices. On 4 dinner plates, equally arrange the lettuce, pork slices, corn, tomatoes, and toasted pecans.

2   To make the **_Toasted Pecan Vinaigrette_**, in a food processor, combine the lemon zest and juice, tarragon vinegar, Dijon mustard, honey, and toasted pecans. Pulse to blend and chop the pecans. With the machine running, slowly add the vegetable oil until thick. Season with salt and pepper.

3   Drizzle the vinaigrette over the salad and serve with any remaining dressing on the side.

TIME-SAVING TIARA TOUCH

You can toast a whole bag of pecans and then store them in the freezer in an airtight container for several months. That way, you'll have them on hand in a jiffy.

Mesquite-Grilled Pasta Salad with Chicken, Peaches, and Cashews

There's comfort in the fact that you can feed your family and friends a delicious and healthy entrée in less than 30 minutes. Grilling boneless, skinless chicken breasts as "paillards," or pieces with the same thickness throughout, gets them done in a flash. The combination of smoky, sweet, tart, mellow, and crunchy in this pasta salad is simply wonderful. To get the mesquite flavor, either throw a handful of soaked mesquite chips onto a charcoal fire (made with mesquite charcoal, preferably) right before grilling, or prepare an aluminum foil packet with holes punched in the top, containing dry mesquite chips or pellets, and place directly on the coals of a charcoal fire or on the grill rack above a gas fire.

SERVES 4

2 large red onions, sliced $1/2$ inch thick

4 boneless, skinless chicken breasts, pounded to $1/2$-inch thickness

Olive oil for brushing

Fine kosher or sea salt and freshly ground black pepper to taste

12 ounces angel hair pasta, cooked according to package directions

2 large, ripe peaches or nectarines, peeled, pitted, and chopped

1 cup roasted salted cashews

$1/2$ cup chopped cilantro

3 tablespoons balsamic vinegar

2 teaspoons Dijon mustard

$1/2$ cup olive oil

1 cup mesquite wood chips or $1/3$ cup mesquite wood pellets (see above)

1   Prepare a hot fire in your grill. For a gas grill, immediately place the packet of dry chips or pellets on the grill grate toward the back of the grill and close the lid. The chips will begin to smoke after 20 minutes. For a charcoal fire, sprinkle moistened wood chips or place a foil packet containing dry wood pellets on the hot coals right before grilling.

2   Brush the onions and chicken with olive oil and season with salt and pepper. Place the chicken and onions on a doubled baking sheet to take out to the grill.

3   Grill the onions on a perforated grill rack, turning once, until softened and slightly charred, about 10 minutes total. Toward the end of that time, grill the chicken breasts, turning once, for 5 minutes total. Place the cooked food on the clean baking sheet to bring inside.

4   In a large bowl, toss the pasta, peaches, cashews, and cilantro together. Cut the grilled chicken breasts into small pieces and toss them with the pasta mixture. In a small bowl, whisk together the vinegar, mustard, and olive oil. Season with salt and pepper. Pour the dressing over the pasta salad and toss again to blend. Serve at room temperature or chilled.

Stir-Grilled Chicken Salad with Asparagus and Blue Cheese

Like a chick flick that even guys like, this main-dish salad pleases both women who want something "lighter" and men who want something with big flavor. If you hold the end of an asparagus spear in one hand and with the other hand bend the spear down to snap it, you'll have a quick way of ensuring that you cook only the tenderest part of the stalk. The flavors in this dish go well with Sauvignon Blanc.

SERVES 4

Dijon Dressing
MAKES ABOUT ²/₃ CUP

¹/₂ cup olive oil

1 tablespoon fresh lemon juice

2 teaspoons Dijon mustard

Fine kosher or sea salt and freshly ground black pepper to taste

1 pound boneless, skinless chicken breast, cut into 1-inch pieces

¹/₂ pound asparagus, ends trimmed and cut on the diagonal into 2-inch pieces

1 medium-size red bell pepper, cored, seeded, and coarsely chopped

1 medium-size red onion, coarsely chopped

2 tablespoons olive oil

Fine kosher or sea salt and freshly ground black pepper to taste

¹/₄ cup oil-packed sun-dried tomatoes, drained, patted dry, and finely chopped

¹/₂ cup (4 ounces) crumbled good-quality blue cheese (Gorgonzola, Maytag, Point Reyes, etc.)

¹/₄ cup finely chopped prosciutto or country ham

4 cups torn salad greens

You've Got Dinner!

CORNBREAD OR CORN MUFFINS

1 Whisk the *Dijon Dressing* ingredients together in a small bowl. Set aside.

2 Prepare a hot fire in your grill. Lightly oil a large grill wok on both sides and set on the hot grill.

3 Place the chicken, asparagus, bell pepper, and onion in a large zipper-top plastic bag. Drizzle with the olive oil, season with salt and pepper, seal the bag, and toss to blend. Place the wok in the sink, pour the contents of the bag into the wok, and let drain. Place the wok on a doubled baking sheet to take out to the grill.

4 In a large serving bowl, combine the sun-dried tomatoes, blue cheese, prosciutto, and salad greens. Set aside.

5 Place the grill wok on the grill and cook, turning the chicken and vegetables with wooden paddles or grill spatulas, for 20 minutes, or until the chicken is cooked through and the vegetables are browned. Place the wok on the clean baking sheet and bring inside.

6 Spoon the grilled chicken mixture onto the salad mixture in the bowl. Pour the dressing over and toss to coat. Divide among 4 plates and serve warm.

Tropical Chicken and Rice Salad with Orange-Coconut Dressing

Grill extra chicken and fruit skewers when you make Tropicana Chicken, Mango, and Pineapple Skewers with Orange-Coconut Marinade (page 158), and this will be a snap. That same marinade also functions as a dressing in this recipe. You can use any kind of salad greens you like. This makes a great warm-weather dinner or a lunch to pack for work. Make a double recipe of the Orange-Coconut Dressing to use a few days later with a mixed greens and mandarin orange salad.

SERVES 4

Orange-Coconut Dressing
MAKES ABOUT 1 CUP

> ¹/₂ **cup regular or light coconut milk**
>
> **1 teaspoon Thai red curry paste, or to taste**
>
> **1 teaspoon orange zest**
>
> ¹/₂ **cup orange juice**
>
>
> **2 cups chopped leftover grilled chicken**
>
> **2 cups chopped leftover grilled tropical fruits**
>
> **2 cups cooked rice**
>
> **2 cups torn fresh greens**

1   Whisk the *Orange-Coconut Dressing* ingredients together.

2   Place the chicken, fruits, rice, and greens in a large serving bowl and toss with the dressing. Cover and chill until ready to serve.

TIME-SAVING TIARA TOUCH

Make one big batch of rice a week instead of several smaller batches. It keeps and reheats well.

We admit it: some of our favorite products come in a can. For dinner on a busy weeknight, we want big, bold flavor quickly. So we look for things that are fire roasted, pre-chopped, and multipurpose. A couple of our favorite brands are Muir Glen and S&W; however, when we can't find these brands, we look for store brands that have added flavor. For instance, we choose tomatoes that are Italian style, knowing that extra herbs have been added for extra flavor, or Ro-Tel tomatoes (available everywhere) that include green chiles for more oomph. Here's our short list of pantry staples we couldn't grill without:

- Anchovies

- Artichoke hearts

- Beans: black, cannellini, garbanzo, and red kidney

- Chicken broth (low-sodium)

- Chipotle peppers in adobo sauce

- Coconut milk

- Green chiles, chopped

- Hearts of palm

- Mandarin oranges

- Tahini

- Tomatoes: fire roasted, with green chiles, and tomato sauce

Grilled Turkey Tenderloin Salad with Green Curry Dressing

Turkey is lean and luscious on the grill, and it can take on just about any flavoring. Try it this way in salad or in lettuce wraps, if you prefer. Thai green curry paste is made up of about 12 different ingredients, including chiles, lemongrass, spices, and herbs. If you made it yourself, it would be time-consuming and expensive, so it's great that you can buy it as a good-quality convenience product in the Asian section of most grocery stores. Combined with coconut milk and rice vinegar or citrus juice, it makes a dynamite dressing for any grilled salad.

SERVES 4

Green Curry Dressing
MAKES ABOUT 1 1/4 CUPS

1 cup regular or light coconut milk

1 1/2 teaspoons green curry paste

2 tablespoons seasoned rice vinegar

Four 4- to 6-ounce turkey breast tenderloin steaks, cut 1/2 inch thick

Olive oil for brushing

Fine kosher or sea salt and freshly ground black pepper to taste

2 cups torn salad greens

15 green onions, chopped (white and green parts)

One 14-ounce can mandarin orange slices, drained and rinsed

One 7-ounce can sliced bamboo shoots, drained

You've Got Dinner!
SMALL BOWLS OF STEAMED RICE, IF YOU WISH

1 To make the *Green Curry Dressing*, combine the coconut milk, green curry paste, and rice vinegar in a small bowl and whisk to blend. Set aside.

2 Prepare a medium to medium-hot fire in your grill.

3   Brush the turkey with olive oil and season with salt and pepper. Place on a doubled baking sheet and take out to the grill.

4   Grill the turkey, turning once, for 12 to 15 minutes total, or until the turkey is no longer pink. Turkey is done when an instant-read thermometer inserted into the meatiest part registers 160°F. Remove it to the clean baking sheet and slice the turkey on the diagonal.

5   In a large bowl, combine the salad greens, green onions, mandarin oranges, and bamboo shoots. Toss with the dressing. Portion the salad onto 4 plates and top with the turkey slices. Serve warm or at room temperature.

Low Country Black-Eyed Pea and Grilled Jumbo Shrimp Salad with Hot Bacon Dressing

This was first concocted as a side dish for our cookbook *Fish & Shellfish, Grilled & Smoked* (The Harvard Common Press, 2002). We like it so much that we've adapted it to use grilled jumbo shrimp and serve as a main-course salad. If you follow our philosophy of leftovers, just make a double batch of the Lime-Basil Shrimp on page 228, and you'll save yourself some time when you make this dish later in the week. We suggest serving your favorite wheat beer with this supper. Because black-eyed peas are supposed to bring good luck, this is perfect for ringing in the New Year—or just a new work week.

SERVES 4 TO 6

3 tablespoons olive oil

2 large cloves garlic, minced

1 small onion, finely diced

1 large red bell pepper, cored, seeded, and finely diced

10 slices smoked bacon, fried crisp and crumbled (reserve the bacon drippings to use instead of the olive oil, if you prefer)

Two 10-ounce packages frozen black-eyed peas, defrosted

3 tablespoons sherry vinegar

1 bunch green onions, chopped

1 pound jumbo or large shrimp, grilled

1 tablespoon freshly ground black pepper

Fine kosher or sea salt to taste

2 heads Boston lettuce, torn into bite-size pieces

You've Got Dinner!

SAUTÉED GREEN BEANS OR OKRA

CORNBREAD OR GRILLED POLENTA SLICES

1 Add the olive oil to a large skillet over medium-high heat. Add the garlic, onion, and bell pepper. Cook, stirring, until softened, about 5 minutes. Stir

in the crumbled bacon and black-eyed peas. Stir in the vinegar, green onions, shrimp, and black pepper. Season with salt and stir to warm the mixture thoroughly.

2   Arrange the lettuce on a serving platter or on individual plates. Spoon the shrimp mixture over the lettuce. Serve warm.

LIFE IN THE FAST LANE: LET THE GROCERY STORE BE YOUR SOUS CHEF

Sometimes chopping, slicing, and dicing can be a therapeutic hands-on activity after a long or stressful day. Sometimes not. When you've had one of "those" days, let the grocery store be your sous chef. Just glide through the salad bar and pick up the already prepared ingredients you need: shredded carrots, chopped vegetables, pitted olives, rinsed lettuce leaves, whole cherry tomatoes, hard-boiled eggs, sliced pepperoni, and shredded or cubed cheese. Pepperoni and cheese can also be found in the deli section, along with pasta and potato salads, three-bean salad, and other ready-made side dishes. You can also buy pre-sliced mushrooms, shredded cabbage, pre-washed and torn lettuce, peeled and cored pineapple, and chopped melon in the produce section. You'll pay a little more, but isn't your sanity worth it?

Grilled Scallop and Heart of Palm Salad with Tarragon Vinaigrette

A warm summer evening begs for a cool and refreshing salad like this one. Grilled scallops, shrimp, squid, or the fish of your choice pairs well with this dressing and will grill quickly, too. We like the flavor of hearts of palm better when chilled, and the contrast with the warm scallops is wonderful. The vinaigrette keeps in the refrigerator for a couple of days, so if you like it, double the batch to serve it with another weeknight salad supper. Serve the salad with your choice of bread and butter and a crisp, dry white wine. Remind your diners to squeeze the citrus wedges over the salad for a final burst of flavor.

SERVES 4

Tarragon Vinaigrette
MAKES ABOUT ²/₃ CUP

- 1 teaspoon chopped red onion
- 1 teaspoon chopped fresh tarragon
- 1 teaspoon chopped Italian parsley
- 1/4 cup fresh lemon juice (from about 2 lemons)
- 1/2 teaspoon Worcestershire sauce
- 1/2 teaspoon kosher or sea salt
- 1/2 teaspoon freshly ground white pepper
- 1/2 cup olive oil

- 2 heads of butter lettuce, torn into bite-size pieces
- 2 large cans hearts of palm, chilled
- 2 large tomatoes, sliced into wedges
- 16 large sea scallops
- 2 tablespoons olive oil
- 1/4 cup chopped Italian parsley
- 1 large red onion, finely chopped

Fine kosher or sea salt and freshly ground black pepper to taste

4 lemon wedges, for garnish

4 lime wedges, for garnish

4 orange wedges, for garnish

1   To make the *Tarragon Vinaigrette*, in a blender or food processor, combine the red onion, tarragon, parsley, lemon juice, Worcestershire sauce, salt, and pepper and pulse to combine. While the blender is running, slowly add the olive oil and blend until thick. Pour into a clean jar and set aside.

2   Prepare a hot fire in your grill. Oil a perforated grill rack and set aside.

3   Arrange the lettuce on 4 dinner plates. Place equal amounts of hearts of palm and tomato wedges on each plate.

4   Combine the scallops and olive oil in a medium-size bowl. Toss to coat the scallops lightly. Place the scallops on the prepared grill rack. Grill for $2^{1}/_{2}$ to 3 minutes per side, turning once.

5   Place 4 grilled scallops on each plate, on top of the salad. Sprinkle with the parsley and red onion. Season with salt and pepper. Garnish the edge of each plate with one wedge of lemon, lime, and orange. Drizzle each plate with 2 to 3 tablespoons of the vinaigrette and serve.

TIME-SAVING TIARA TOUCH

Make a double batch of the Tarragon Vinaigrette up to 2 days ahead and store in the refrigerator. It's dynamite on any grilled fish.

Savory Sandwiches, Burgers, and Pizzas

Sandwiches, burgers, and pizzas on the grill have an incomparable flavor. With such great taste, they can easily be the main attraction for a weeknight dinner.

With artisan breads and rolls more readily available than ever, you can enjoy a crusty, slightly sour, and naturally leavened loaf. (Learn how to make your own in Judith's *Prairie Home Breads* [The Harvard Common Press, 2001], but save that for a weekend.) Slice a whole loaf lengthwise, fill it with wonderful sandwich ingredients, slather it with a savory butter or drench it in a flavorful sofrito mixture (see page 94), then grill. Many grocery stores have in-store bakeries producing good-quality artisan breads. Larger cities will have specialty bakeries with naturally leavened breads and rolls as their calling cards. Even the frozen-food section of Super Target grocery stores has frozen artisan bread, ready to be thawed, baked, and enjoyed.

In addition to artisan breads, the BBQ Queens also favor frozen bread dough for a quick pizza base during the week. Many grocery stores sell their own freshly made pizza dough in the refrigerated section. We also like fresh pita bread, lavash, and other ready-made flatbreads for quick, light pizzas. Just brush these with olive oil, sprinkle with herbs or a bit of cheese, and sizzle on the grill.

A really good bread can also be a great vehicle for making leftover grilled foods interesting and new again. Pile on the grilled vegetables and slather on some goat cheese, or slice up the grilled steak and some juicy tomatoes, for a delicious sandwich. Remember to grill extra hamburgers to wrap and refrigerate for meals later in the week, then zap them in the microwave to reheat. The benefit of a leftover medium to medium-rare burger is that even when you microwave it, the burger stays juicy.

Grilled Italian Garden Sandwich

This easy sandwich makes for a great casual meal. It's so easy to put together, you can have your kids assemble the sandwich, if you wish. Feel free to substitute herbed cream cheese for goat cheese, if that is what your family prefers. While the sandwich is grilling, you could also think ahead and grill some shrimp, chicken breasts, or vegetables for meals later in the week. On a medium instead of a hot fire, they will take several minutes longer to grill but should be done by the time your sandwich has heated through.

SERVES 4

1 large loaf fresh **Italian or French bread**

Olive oil for brushing

3 tablespoons prepared pesto, or more to taste

9 ounces soft goat cheese

6 large Roma tomatoes, thinly sliced lengthwise

1 medium-size cucumber, thinly sliced

$1/2$ cup pitted and sliced olives, such as Kalamata

$1/2$ cup store-bought roasted red pepper strips

$1/2$ cup chopped store-bought marinated artichoke hearts

Freshly ground black pepper to taste

You've Got Dinner!

GRILLED OR OVEN-BAKED POTATO WEDGES OR POTATO SALAD

GREEN SALAD

1   Cut the Italian bread in half lengthwise and turn the top half over so that the crust side is on the counter. With your fingers or a fork, hollow out about one-third of the top half of the bread and discard or reserve for another use. Brush the bottom half with olive oil, then spread the pesto and goat cheese on it. Layer on the tomatoes, cucumber, olives, roasted red pepper, and artichoke hearts. Season with pepper. Brush the hollowed top half of the bread with olive oil and place on top of the sandwich fillings. Wrap well in heavy-duty aluminum foil.

2   Prepare a medium fire in your grill.

3   Grill the sandwich, covered, turning once, until heated through, 20 to 25 minutes. Cut into quarters and serve warm or at room temperature.

TIME-SAVING TIARA TOUCH

You may assemble the sandwich, wrap it in aluminum foil, and store it in the refrigerator in the morning, for dinner that night.

Grilled Falafel Pocket Burgers with Homemade Hummus

We adapted this recipe from one by fellow Harvard Common Press authors Jane Murphy and Liz Yeh Singh, whose *The Great Big Burger Book* (2003) should be on your shelf! Made from chickpeas and livened up with garlic, spices, fresh herbs, and lemon juice, these veggie burgers taste great sizzled on the grill, then stuffed into a grilled pita pocket. Along with the hummus, add the fixin's of your choice: thinly sliced cucumber, tomato, and sweet onion along with grated carrot, leaf lettuce, or whatever strikes your fancy. Save any extra hummus to serve with Grilled Pita Bread with Grilled Baba Ghanoush and Fresh Cucumber (page 32).

SERVES 4

Homemade Hummus

MAKES ABOUT 3 CUPS

> One 15-ounce can chickpeas, rinsed and well drained
>
> 4 cloves garlic, minced
>
> 1/2 cup tahini (sesame seed paste, available in the Middle Eastern section of the grocery store or at health food stores)
>
> 1/2 cup fresh lemon juice (from about 4 lemons)
>
> 1 1/2 teaspoons freshly ground black pepper

> One 15-ounce can chickpeas, rinsed and well drained
>
> 3 cloves garlic, minced
>
> 2 teaspoons ground cumin
>
> 1 teaspoon ground coriander
>
> 1/2 cup tightly packed fresh flat-leaf parsley leaves
>
> 1/2 cup tightly packed fresh cilantro leaves
>
> 3 tablespoons olive oil, plus more for brushing
>
> 1/2 cup chopped green onion (white part with some of the green)

You've Got Dinner!

BLANCHED BABY CARROTS TOSSED WITH YOUR FAVORITE LEMONY VINAIGRETTE

½ **cup toasted bread crumbs**

1 fresh jalapeño pepper, seeded and chopped

1 large egg

Fine kosher or sea salt and freshly ground black pepper to taste

2 pita bread rounds, each cut into 2 pockets

Sliced cucumber, tomato, sweet onion, grated carrots, and leaf lettuce, for toppings

1   Combine the *Homemade Hummus* ingredients in the bowl of a food processor and puree. Set aside. (This can be made up to 2 days ahead.)

2   In the same food processor (no need to clean it), process the chickpeas, garlic, cumin, coriander, parsley, cilantro, and 3 tablespoons of olive oil until the mixture forms a thick paste. Transfer to a large bowl and blend in the green onion, bread crumbs, jalapeño, and egg, then season to taste with salt and pepper. Form the mixture into four ½-inch-thick patties. Brush each patty and the pita bread pockets with olive oil and place on a baking sheet to take out to the grill.

3   Prepare a hot fire in your grill. Oil a perforated grill rack and place on the grill grate.

4   Grill the patties on the prepared grill rack for 4 to 8 minutes total, turning once, or until golden brown. At the same time, grill the pita bread pockets on both sides until warmed through. Place a burger in each pocket. Add hummus and the toppings of your choice.

Wood-Grilled Brie Burgers with Grilled Onions and Tomato-Avocado Relish

Okay, anybody can grill a hamburger. This recipe shows you how to grill a *great* hamburger. This decadent version of a traditional cheeseburger has style and panache (just like the BBQ Queens!) as well as great flavor. Adding moistened wood chips or dry wood pellets to the fire gives you more of a smoky taste. On a gas grill, use a foil packet with holes poked through the top to enclose 1 cup of dry wood chips or $1/3$ cup dry wood pellets. On a charcoal grill, add moistened wood chips or a foil packet containing dry wood pellets directly to the coals after the fire is hot. Don't be afraid to grill a whole baby Brie: it's a lot easier than you think. You just have to pay attention and take it off the grill the minute you see the cheese starting to ooze out of the rind. The relish is your vegetable and salad all rolled into one. (You didn't hear it from us, but any Brie that oozes out of your burger would be even more decadent scooped up with French fries.)

SERVES 4

Tomato-Avocado Relish
MAKES ABOUT 4 CUPS

 1 pint cherry tomatoes, cut in half

 1 large ripe avocado, pitted and diced

 2 tablespoons finely chopped red onion

 1 jalapeño pepper, seeded and diced

 2 cloves garlic, minced

 $1/4$ cup finely minced fresh Italian parsley

 2 tablespoons extra virgin olive oil

 2 tablespoons fresh lime juice

 Fine kosher or sea salt and freshly ground black pepper to taste

 1 cup wood chips or $1/3$ cup wood pellets (see above)

 1 pound ground chuck, formed into four 1-inch-thick patties

1 large red onion, peeled and cut into ¹/₂-inch-thick slices

One 6- to 8-ounce wheel of baby Brie cheese

Olive oil for brushing

Fine kosher or sea salt and freshly ground black pepper to taste

4 seeded hamburger buns, kaiser rolls, or ciabattini

1 Combine the *Tomato-Avocado Relish* ingredients in a large bowl. Cover and set aside.

2 Prepare a hot fire in your grill. Oil a perforated grill rack and place on the grill. If using a charcoal grill, throw moistened wood chips or a foil packet poked with holes containing dry wood pellets directly on the coals right before you want to grill. If using a gas grill, enclose dry wood chips or pellets in a metal smoker box or in a foil packet poked with holes. Place on the grill grate directly over the fire. Heat for 20 minutes until the wood begins to smoke, then you're ready to wood-grill.

3 Place the patties on a plate on a baking sheet. Brush the red onion slices and the Brie with olive oil on both sides. Season with salt and pepper. Place on the baking sheet to take out to the grill.

4 Grill the onions on the prepared perforated grill rack, turning once, for 8 minutes. Grill the burgers directly on the grate, turning once, for 7 minutes for medium. Grill the Brie on the prepared perforated grill rack for 5 to 7 minutes, or until the cheese is *just beginning* to ooze out of the rind.

5 Place each burger on the bottom half of a bun and top with the grilled onions. Cut the Brie into 4 wedges and place a wedge on top of each burger. Cover with the top portion of the bun and serve immediately with the relish on the side.

Grilled Steak Sandwiches with Aioli, Tomatoes, and Arugula

With extra grilled flank, rib-eye, or sirloin steak on hand, maybe from Latin Lover's Carne Asada with Orange and Red Onion Mojo (page 108), you can create a signature steak sandwich for a casual meal that will please everyone. Use our Quick Aioli, Portuguese Aioli, or leftover Gorgonzola Sauce to dress it up. If you like, slice a large red onion into $^1/_2$-inch-thick slices, brush with olive oil, and grill or broil for about 5 minutes on each side. Put those on the sandwiches, too.

SERVES 4

4 kaiser rolls or ciabattini

1 recipe Quick Aioli (page 192), Portuguese Aioli (page 86), or Gorgonzola Sauce (page 114)

About 1 pound leftover grilled steak, sliced

2 large tomatoes, sliced

2 cups baby arugula or salad greens

You've Got Dinner!

CARROT AND CELERY STICKS, STEAMED GREEN BEANS, OR GIARDINIERA

Cut the rolls in half lengthwise and slather both cut sides with aioli. On the bottom half of each roll, layer slices of leftover grilled steak, sliced tomatoes, and baby greens, then top with the other half of the roll. Serve.

TIME-SAVING TIARA TOUCH

It's easy to create your own basic quick aioli to go with any grilled food. Start with 1 cup good-quality mayonnaise, then add minced garlic and fresh citrus juice to taste.

In this book, we give you lots of quick sauces that are perfect for a busy weeknight meal. Most sauces involve either just stirring ingredients together in a bowl or cooking them quickly in a pan. There's one, however, that "cooks" in a blender. This sauce goes well with grilled fish, shellfish, and vegetables. It's also great to spoon over foods you cook in a packet (see pages 184 and 194). You can keep the leftover sauce, covered, in the refrigerator for up to 3 days, and it tastes great warm or cold. If you have concerns about using raw eggs, you may use the equivalent amount of egg substitute.

MAKES ABOUT 1 ½ CUPS

6 large egg yolks

1 teaspoon dry mustard (we like Colman's)

2 tablespoons fresh lemon juice

1 cup (2 sticks) unsalted butter, melted and still hot

¼ teaspoon cayenne pepper, or to your taste

Fine kosher or sea salt to taste

Place the egg yolks, mustard, and lemon juice in a blender or food processor and puree until smooth. Drizzle in the hot melted butter, with the blender on low speed or pulsing the food processor, until the sauce thickens. Add the cayenne and season with salt. Keep warm over a pan of hot, not boiling, water until ready to serve.

Grilled Supreme Pizza Loaf

The same ingredients that go into a supreme pizza can taste wonderful in a grilled sandwich. Now that you can buy already cooked sausage crumbles, preparation is that much easier. If you can't find the precooked sausage, substitute Canadian bacon or ham, or use sausage you've already cooked. If you want to be thrifty, you can save the scooped-out insides of the bread, let them dry for a day or two, and grate them for homemade bread crumbs. You can also prepare this sandwich earlier in the day, wrap it in foil, and refrigerate it, so all you have left to do later is grill it.

SERVES 4

1 large loaf fresh **Italian or French bread**

Olive oil for brushing

$^2/_3$ cup **pizza sauce** of your choice

$^1/_2$ cup **pepperoni** slices

$^1/_2$ cup cooked, crumbled **Italian or regular pork or turkey sausage**

$^1/_2$ cup finely chopped **red onion**

$^1/_2$ cup finely chopped **green bell pepper**

$^1/_2$ cup pitted, sliced **olives**, such as **Kalamata**

One 4-ounce can sliced **mushrooms**, drained

2 cups shredded or sliced **mozzarella or provolone cheese**, or a combination

You've Got Dinner!

CHOPPED ROMAINE
LETTUCE, ENDIVE,
CUCUMBERS, AND CELERY
TOSSED WITH CAESAR
DRESSING

1   Cut the Italian bread in half lengthwise and turn the top half over so that the crust side is on the counter. With your fingers or a fork, hollow out about one-third of the top half of the bread and set aside. Spread the bottom half with the pizza sauce. Layer on the pepperoni, sausage, onion, bell pepper, olives, and mushrooms. Sprinkle with the cheese. Place the top over the sandwich fillings. Brush the top and bottom of the bread with olive oil. Wrap well in heavy-duty aluminum foil.

2 Prepare a medium fire in your grill.

3 Grill the loaf, covered, turning once, until heated through, 20 to 25 minutes. Cut into quarters and serve hot.

TIME-SAVING TIARA TOUCH

Smoked turkey or other deli meat or grilled chicken from the salad bar can be substituted for the sausage in this sandwich.

Umbrian Olive Panini with Fontina and Prosciutto al Mattone

The Umbria region in central Italy is known for its fine olives and olive oils, and the olives are the star in this grilled sandwich. Since focaccia comes in all different sizes, it's hard to specify a size, so just use enough for four sandwiches according to your appetite. Although Italians would use a young and sliceable pecorino instead of fontina, a young pecorino can be a challenge to find in this country. If you can get it, then use it and rejoice! *Al mattone* refers to a brick, which means you press the panini down as they grill. To do this, you can use two bricks covered with foil, a heavy cast-iron skillet, or a bacon press as a weight, or simply press down hard on the panini with heavy-duty grill spatulas.

SERVES 4

4 slices focaccia, sliced in half horizontally

Olive oil for brushing

8 ounces fontina cheese, sliced

1 cup brine- or oil-cured black olives, pitted and chopped

8 thin slices prosciutto

You've Got Dinner!

BABY SPINACH AND NAVEL ORANGE SALAD OR SLICED TOMATOES SPRINKLED WITH FRESH BASIL AND UMBRIAN OLIVE OIL

1. Brush all sides of each focaccia slice with olive oil. On the bottom portion of each sandwich, place the cheese, then the olives, then the prosciutto. Top with the remaining focaccia slices. Place the panini on a baking sheet to take out to the grill.

2. Prepare a medium-hot fire in your grill. Have your weight of choice by the grill.

3. Place each panino on the grill rack and weight or press down. Grill for 3 to 4 minutes on each side, or until you have good grill marks and the cheese has melted. If necessary to weight them down properly, grill these one at a time.

4. Slice each panino in half and serve hot.

LIFE IN THE FAST LANE: PIZZA TOPPINGS

 Yummy leftover grilled veggies and meats make perfect pizza toppings. A stop at a great gourmet shop or ethnic grocery store can also yield inspiration to create over-the-top pizzas that will make you the talk of the neighborhood. Buy a ready-made crust such as Boboli, flatbread, focaccia, or pita, or buy pre-made fresh dough from your grocer's refrigerated section. Keep your pantry stocked with tomato-based sauces that are mixed with capers, olives, sun-dried tomatoes, or red peppers. Buy pre-made relishes such as artichoke, pesto, tapenade, and roasted pepper. Keep fresh herbs on hand, or grow them in your garden or on your windowsill. Then get creative and blend together your own signature combos. Here are a few ideas to get you started. Slather your pizza crust of choice with olive oil, Dijon mustard, a tomato-based sauce, or even thinly spread soft cheese such as Boursin or creamy goat cheese, then add:

- **Fresh corn off the cob, chopped tomatoes, basil leaves, and fontina cheese**

- **Grilled pork, caramelized onions, and pepper Jack cheese**

- **Grilled shrimp, black or green olives, roasted red peppers, and goat cheese**

- **Thinly sliced grilled steak, grape tomatoes, artichoke hearts, and Asiago cheese**

- **Shaved ham, your favorite chutney, and cheddar cheese**

- **Grilled salmon, sun-dried tomatoes, fresh herbs, and Boursin cheese**

- **Thin slices of fresh tomato and red onion, black olives, basil leaves, and capers**

- **Anchovies, caramelized onions, minced garlic, and oil-cured olives**

- **Baby spinach leaves, basil leaves, fresh or dried figs, and Parmesan cheese**

Grilled Chicken, Roasted Red Pepper, Red Onion, and Artichoke Pizzas

When it's pizza night at your house, change things up a bit. In the time it takes a ho-hum pizza to bake in the oven, you can prepare a great grilled one. Just grill the chicken, then assemble and grill the pizzas. If you have leftover grilled chicken from another night, you can skip that step (that's why we preach the value of leftovers). Feel free to substitute whatever vegetables your family likes—just don't pile them on the pizzas. These are meant to be thin, so that they will cook quickly.

SERVES 4

I pound fresh or frozen bread or pizza dough, at room temperature

Cornmeal for dusting

Olive oil for brushing

4 boneless, skinless chicken breasts

2 cups shredded low-fat mozzarella cheese

2 tablespoons olive oil

I teaspoon dried oregano

I teaspoon dried basil

2 cloves garlic, minced

$1/4$ cup freshly grated Parmesan cheese

I cup chopped red onion

I cup store-bought roasted red pepper strips, patted dry

One 15-ounce can artichoke hearts, drained and sliced

1   Prepare a hot fire in your grill.

2   Cut the dough into 4 equal portions. Sprinkle cornmeal on a clean, flat surface and roll each portion of dough out to about an 8-inch circle. Brush both sides of the dough with olive oil and place on baking sheets. Set aside.

3 Brush the chicken breasts with olive oil and place on a plate. In a medium-size bowl, combine the mozzarella, 2 tablespoons of olive oil, herbs, garlic, and Parmesan. Place the onion, roasted red pepper, and artichoke hearts in a small bowl. Put the plate and the two bowls on a baking sheet, add a paring knife, and take everything out to the grill.

4 Grill the chicken breasts for 3 to 4 minutes per side, or until firm to the touch, then remove and slice on the diagonal into 1-inch-thick strips. Grill the pizza rounds until the dough starts to bubble and blister, turn with grill tongs, and grill on the other side, 4 to 5 minutes total. Return the pizza rounds to their baking sheets. Arrange the chicken strips on each round and top each with one-fourth each of the cheese mixture, onions, roasted red pepper strips, and artichoke hearts. Place the pizzas on the indirect side of the grill, close the lid, and cook for 3 to 5 minutes, or until the cheese has melted. Transfer to the baking sheets, bring inside, and slice and serve immediately.

Deli Pizza

Buy these goodies at the local deli for a delicious and quick weeknight grilled pizza that you can assemble in minutes. By all means, change the meat choices if your family prefers something else, and buy the smaller individual-size Boboli crusts if you want to let everyone make individual pizzas. You can set up all the goodies buffet-style and let each person choose.

SERVES 4

I cup spicy Italian tomato sauce

I large or 2 medium-size **Boboli** pizza crusts

I medium-size tomato, thinly sliced

$^1/_4$ red onion, thinly sliced

4 slices fennel salami

4 slices **Genoa** salami

4 slices prosciutto

6 slices provolone cheese

12 basil leaves

$^1/_2$ cup sliced black olives

1   Prepare a medium fire in your grill.

2   Spread the tomato sauce evenly over the pizza crust. Layer the tomato and onion slices on top.

3   Thinly slice the meats and cheese by stacking them on top of each other and cutting strips about $^1/_8$ to $^1/_4$ inch thick. Scatter the strips over the pizza. Arrange the basil leaves on top, pressing them down. Sprinkle with the olives.

4   Place the pizza directly over the fire for 3 to 4 minutes to heat the bread. Move to the indirect side of the grill and close the lid. Let the pizza heat through for another 5 to 8 minutes. Serve hot.

LIFE IN THE FAST LANE: SURPRISE PACKAGES

 One of the easiest and least stressful dinner techniques is to assemble a foil packet of food destined for your grill. You want food that will steam in the packets and look and taste great. Fish, pork medallions, thin boneless chicken or turkey cutlets, and ham work well. (Beef tends to turn an unappetizing gray color.) Beyond the specific *en papillote* recipes we provide for you throughout the book, here are a few more ideas to try:

- Ham slices with sliced new potatoes, sliced onions, and shredded kale

- Cod fillets with baby spinach, chopped tomato, and Quick Aioli (page 192) after you open the packet

- Turkey cutlets with sliced sweet potatoes, sliced fresh apple or pear, and mango chutney

- Salmon steaks with shredded napa cabbage, sliced mushrooms, and Blender Hollandaise (page 75) after you open the packet

- Pork tenderloin medallions with shredded red cabbage and apples

- Chicken breast with sliced portobello mushrooms, fresh herbs, and cream

Grilled Chicken Caesar on Ciabatta

Okay, we've all had a grilled chicken Caesar salad. Been there, done that. Here's a fresh take on it—grilled chicken on wonderful artisan ciabatta bread with a zippy Caesar dressing that is good on all kinds of grilled food. If you have leftover grilled chicken breast, this recipe becomes even easier. If not, a paillard or chicken breast pounded thin takes only minutes to cook on a hot grill. Use a vegetable peeler to shave shards of Parmesan for the sandwich.

SERVES 4

Caesar Dressing
MAKES ABOUT ²/3 CUP

5 tablespoons mayonnaise

I to 2 teaspoons anchovy paste (we like to buy it in a small tube, at better grocery stores)

I clove garlic, minced, or more to taste

I teaspoon Dijon mustard

I tablespoon fresh lemon juice

Fine kosher or sea salt and freshly ground black pepper to taste

¹/3 cup freshly grated Parmesan cheese

You've Got Dinner!

MARINATED GREEN
BEAN SALAD

FRESH SLICED
STRAWBERRIES
DRIZZLED WITH
BALSAMIC VINEGAR

2 loaves ciabatta or 4 ciabattini (ciabatta rolls), sliced in half lengthwise

Olive oil for brushing

4 boneless, skinless chicken breasts, pounded to a ¹/2-inch thickness

Fine kosher or sea salt and freshly ground black pepper to taste

Small wedge of Parmesan cheese for shaving

2 cups torn romaine lettuce leaves

I   Combine the ingredients for the *Caesar Dressing* in a small bowl and set aside. If you like your Caesar a little zippier, add more anchovy paste and garlic.

2   Prepare a hot fire in your grill.

3   Brush the cut sides of the ciabatta with olive oil and place on a baking sheet. Brush the chicken breasts with olive oil on both sides and season with salt and pepper. Place on a plate on the baking sheet to bring out to the grill.

4   Grill the chicken, turning once, for 5 minutes total. Grill the ciabatta, cut sides down, until you have good grill marks, 1 to 2 minutes. Place the cooked chicken breasts on the clean baking sheet with the ciabatta and bring indoors.

5   Slather all the grilled sides of the ciabatta with the dressing. Place the chicken breasts on the bottom half of the bread, shave some Parmesan over the chicken, then top with lettuce and the top half of the bread. If you're using a loaf of ciabatta, you'll have 2 chicken breasts on each loaf, so cut each loaf in half to get 2 sandwiches. If you're using ciabattini, you'll use 1 breast for each roll. Serve immediately.

TIME-SAVING TIARA TOUCH

Keep good quality Italian-style dressing in your pantry. It's good for quick marinating, basting, and drizzling. Add anchovy paste to Italian dressing and you've got a quick Caesar dressing!

Grilled Chicken and Vegetable Sandwiches with Portuguese Aioli

We recommend that you use ciabatta or kaiser rolls instead of ho-hum grocery store buns for this. Grill double the amount of chicken that you need in this recipe and you'll save yourself some time later in the week, when you can whip together Grilled Chicken Pasta with Tomatoes, Fresh Thyme, and Brine-Cured Olives (page 160).

SERVES 4

Portuguese Aioli
MAKES ABOUT $^1/_2$ CUP

- $^1/_2$ **cup regular or low-fat mayonnaise**
- **2 cloves garlic, minced**
- $^1/_2$ **teaspoon hot pepper sauce**
- **1 teaspoon freshly grated orange zest**
- $^1/_2$ **teaspoon smoked or sweet Hungarian paprika**

- **4 boneless, skinless chicken breasts or 8 boneless chicken thighs, pounded to a $^1/_2$-inch thickness**
- **4 medium-size red bell peppers**
- **1 large red onion, cut into 1-inch-thick slices**
- $^1/_2$ **cup olive oil, plus more for brushing**
- **Kosher or sea salt and freshly ground black pepper to taste**
- **Juice of 1 small lemon (about 1$^1/_2$ tablespoons)**
- **4 small ciabatta rolls, kaiser rolls, or other sturdy sandwich bread**
- **1 cup mixed green lettuce or baby arugula**

You've Got Dinner!

GRILLED CORN ON THE COB

STEAMED POTATOES TOSSED WITH AIOLI

1 Mix together the **Portuguese Aioli** ingredients in a small bowl. Cover and refrigerate until ready to serve.

2 Prepare a hot fire in your grill.

3   Place the chicken on one baking sheet and the peppers and onion slices on another. In a small bowl, combine the $\frac{1}{2}$ cup olive oil and the salt, pepper, and lemon juice. Brush this mixture on the peppers and onions, and then on the chicken. Take both sheets out to the grill.

4   Grill the chicken for 5 minutes total, turning once. Grill the peppers, turning several times, until the skin is charred and blistered all over. Grill the onion slices for 10 minutes total, turning once halfway through the cooking. Transfer the cooked food to the baking sheet you used for the peppers and onions. Trim away the cores and seeds from the peppers.

5   To assemble the sandwiches, brush the cut sides of the rolls with olive oil and spread with the aioli. On the bottom of each roll place a piece of chicken, then some red pepper, then grilled onion slices. Top each with $\frac{1}{4}$ cup lettuce, then place the top of the roll over the lettuce and serve.

Grilled Chicken on Blue Cheese–Buttered Hoagies with Blue Cheese Slaw

Don't be afraid to invite company for this supper. These simple ingredients yield *beaucoup* flavor. After you try this, you'll want to grill extra chicken all the time to have on hand for these sandwiches. We like to toast the sandwich bun long enough for the butter and blue cheese to melt into the bread and get nice and crispy. The consistency of a hoagie roll is perfect, but other choices could be a kaiser roll or ciabatta. It isn't as good with sliced sandwich bread, so make sure your choice is some kind of bun. If you want to add arugula or spinach to the sandwich, be our guest. The blue cheese butter can easily adapt to become a feta butter, if you like.

MAKES 4 SERVINGS

$^1/_2$ **cup (1 stick) unsalted butter, softened**

$^1/_2$ **cup (4 ounces) crumbled blue cheese**

4 hoagie rolls, sliced in half lengthwise

4 boneless, skinless chicken breasts, grilled

Blue Cheese Slaw

4 cups shredded cabbage

$^1/_2$ **cup (4 ounces) crumbled blue cheese**

2 tablespoons fresh lemon juice

$^1/_3$ **cup vegetable oil**

1 tablespoon Dijon mustard

1 tablespoon sugar

$^1/_4$ **teaspoon kosher or sea salt**

$^1/_2$ **teaspoon freshly ground black pepper**

You've Got Dinner!

MARINATED THREE-BEAN SALAD

VINAIGRETTE POTATO SALAD

1   Prepare a medium fire in your grill.

2   In a small bowl, combine the softened butter and crumbled blue cheese. Liberally spread the blue cheese butter on each cut side of the hoagie rolls. Place a grilled chicken breast on each bun. Wrap each sandwich in a square of heavy-duty aluminum foil. Place on the grill and close the lid. Grill for about 20 minutes, or until the sandwiches feel hot all the way through.

3   While the sandwiches are grilling, make the coleslaw. Place the shredded cabbage and blue cheese in a large bowl. In a small bowl, combine the lemon juice, vegetable oil, mustard, sugar, salt, and pepper. Whisk to blend, pour over the cabbage, and toss well to coat. Serve immediately alongside the sandwiches.

TIME-SAVING TIARA TOUCH

You can buy packages of pre-shredded cabbage in the produce department of your grocery store, which will save you from having to shred whole cabbage with a food processor or by hand.

Tandoori Turkey Burgers with Onion, Tomato, and Cucumber Raita

The BBQ Queens love a juicy grilled beef burger with all the fixin's as much as the next person. But sometimes the old standbys just get, well, old. This burger is juicy and delicious, too, as well as leaner and healthier than the standard hamburger. Now that ground turkey is so easy to find at the grocery store, making these burgers is a breeze. You can serve the raita both as a topping for the burgers and as a side dip with a platter of crudités.

SERVES 4

Onion, Tomato, and Cucumber Raita
MAKES ABOUT 3 CUPS

$^1/_2$ cup chopped green onion (white and green parts)

1 cup chopped and seeded cucumber

1 large tomato, peeled, seeded, and chopped

2 tablespoons chopped fresh cilantro

1 cup plain yogurt (low-fat is okay, but do not use fat-free)

1 pound ground turkey

$^1/_4$ cup fine, dry bread crumbs

2 tablespoons plain yogurt (low-fat is okay, but do not use fat-free)

1 teaspoon turmeric

1 teaspoon ground coriander

1 teaspoon ground cumin

1 teaspoon fine kosher or sea salt

4 seeded hamburger buns

Shredded lettuce and chopped tomato, for toppings

You've Got Dinner!

PLATTER OF CRUDITÉS, SUCH AS CARROTS, CELERY, RADISHES, AND YELLOW BELL PEPPERS

RED AND GREEN GRAPES

1 Combine the *Onion, Tomato, and Cucumber Raita* ingredients in a large bowl and set aside.

2 Brush the grill rack with oil. Prepare a medium fire in your grill.

3 In a large bowl, combine the ground turkey, bread crumbs, yogurt, and spices until well blended. Form into four ³/₄-inch-thick patties. Place the patties on a plate set on a baking sheet to take out to the grill. Place the buns on the baking sheet.

4 Grill the patties, turning once, for 14 to 18 minutes, or until no longer pink inside and an instant-read thermometer registers 165°F in the center of a patty. During the last minutes of grilling, toast the buns, cut sides down, on the grill rack.

5 To serve, place a patty on each bun. Top with shredded lettuce, chopped tomatoes, and a dollop of raita.

TIME-SAVING TIARA TOUCH

You'll likely have some leftover raita, so why not grill a couple of extra burgers while you're at it? Microwaved for lunch later in the week, they'll keep all of their juicy goodness.

Grilled Catfish on Buttered Sourdough with Scallion Mayonnaise

The BBQ Queens are true fans of farm-raised catfish. The farm-raised fish is a top feeder, and the diet that it is fed produces a mildly sweet, firm-textured fish that is perfect for the grill. We like to spice it up and serve it with something lush and creamy, like the Blue Cheese Slaw on page 88. If you'd like a different side dish, try this entrée with the seasonal vegetable of your choice: grilled or steamed asparagus in the spring, grilled zucchini and summer squash in the summer, or baked butternut squash in the colder months, topped with a dollop of the scallion mayonnaise. Better double the mayo recipe!

SERVES 4

Scallion Mayonnaise
MAKES ABOUT ²/₃ CUP

1/3 cup regular or low-fat mayonnaise

8 scallions (white and green parts), chopped

Zest and juice of 1 lemon

2 teaspoons chopped fresh mint or basil

Four 6- to 8-ounce farm-raised catfish fillets

1 tablespoon olive oil

2 teaspoons spicy barbecue rub of your choice

4 thick slices good-quality sourdough bread

4 teaspoons unsalted butter, softened

2 cups chopped arugula or mesclun greens

1 lemon, cut into 4 wedges, for garnish

You've Got Dinner!
BLUE CHEESE SLAW
(PAGE 88)

1   In a small bowl, combine all the ingredients for the *Scallion Mayonnaise*. Stir to blend and set aside.

2   Prepare a hot fire in your grill.

3   Rinse the catfish fillets and pat dry. Place on a doubled baking sheet, lightly coat with the olive oil, and season with the spicy barbecue rub.

4   Toast the sourdough bread and butter each slice with 1 teaspoon of the softened butter. Set aside on 4 plates.

5   Take the catfish to the grill and grill for about 3 to 4 minutes on each side, turning once. Transfer the cooked catfish to the clean baking sheet. To serve, lightly spread some scallion mayonnaise on each piece of buttered toast. Sprinkle $1/2$ cup of the arugula on top of each piece, followed by a fillet and an extra dollop of the mayonnaise. Serve immediately with a wedge of lemon.

TIME-SAVING TIARA TOUCH

Feel free to mix up your own spicy barbecue rub if you have a favorite recipe, but there are many good pre-made seasoning mixes available in the spice section of most supermarkets.

Sofrito Grilled Bread and Shrimp

Sometimes, dining in little bites is just what you want to do. The idea of tapas or meze as a full dinner is possible on a busy weeknight if you have some ready-made ingredients on hand. Feel free to complement this dish with a jar of tapenade or marinated feta, a store-bought marinated vegetable salad, or whatever else strikes your fancy. Sofrito is a sautéed vegetable seasoning mixture from Latin America. It typically contains garlic, onion, bell pepper, cilantro, and sometimes tomatoes or ham, although the recipe varies from family to family. Try this dish with a cold beer or a chilled, dry fino sherry.

SERVES 4

Sofrito

MAKES ABOUT 1 1/2 CUPS

3 tablespoons olive oil

1 cup chopped red bell pepper

1/2 cup chopped onion

1/4 cup packed fresh cilantro sprigs, washed well and patted dry

2 cloves garlic, minced

1 teaspoon dried oregano, crumbled

1/2 teaspoon ground cumin

Fine sea or kosher salt and freshly ground black pepper to taste

1 large loaf country-style bread, cut into 1-inch-thick slices

1 pound large shrimp, peeled and deveined

You've Got Dinner!

CANNELLINI BEANS MASHED WITH OLIVE OIL AND ROSEMARY

SLICED TOMATOES

1 To make the *Sofrito*, heat the olive oil in a small heavy saucepan over medium-high heat. Add the bell pepper, onion, cilantro, garlic, oregano, and cumin. Cook, stirring, for 5 minutes, or until much of the liquid has

evaporated. Season with salt and pepper and set aside to cool slightly. Puree the sofrito in a food processor or blender.

2 Prepare a medium-hot fire in your grill, then oil the grill grates and a perforated grill rack.

3 Divide the sofrito in half. Spread half the sofrito on one side of each bread slice. Place the shrimp in a zipper-top plastic bag and pour the remaining sofrito over them, seal the bag, and toss to coat the shrimp. Place the bread and bag of shrimp on a baking sheet and take out to the grill.

4 Grill the bread, sofrito side down, until golden brown with good grill marks, 2 to 3 minutes. Transfer to the baking sheet. Place the shrimp on the perforated grill rack and grill, turning, until pink and opaque all the way through, about 5 minutes total. To serve, divide the bread and shrimp among 4 plates.

TIME-SAVING TIARA TOUCH

You can make our version of sofrito up to 2 days ahead. Refrigerate it in an airtight container.

Great Grilled Steak

For a busy weeknight dinner entrée, there is nothing quite as easy as beef. In this chapter, we've focused on those cuts of beef that grill quickly, for delicious no-fuss dinners when your week is already hectic. From the boneless, flat-cut flank, hanger, or skirt steaks to the 2-inch-thick sirloin—with all the $^3/_4$- to 1-inch-thick rib-eyes, porterhouses, strips, and T-bones in between—a grilled steak satisfies in more ways than one. Save the roasts and briskets for the weekend.

Why beef? First of all, steak grills in minutes over high heat. The BBQ Queens prefer our steaks (and burgers) a little charred on the outside, and medium-rare on the inside, so we like a hot fire. You can achieve medium or medium-rare beef over a hot fire as well by grilling slightly longer; if you prefer less char, just lower the heat a bit. We also like to grill vegetables at the same time: vegetable skewers, asparagus spears, strips of zucchini or eggplant, or even stir-grilled cherry tomatoes. Second, beef (as well as chicken and pork) is great for a busy weeknight because it grills quickly, so you can prepare a great meal *and* end up with wonderful leftovers. You can do two things at once. Don't we love

that? Recycle leftover grilled steak into delicious sandwiches, salads, pizzas, or even a savory steak soup. Remember: the time you save *not* preparing another dinner could be your own. (On the déjà vu dinner evening, you could be sipping a glass of wine and thumbing through *O* magazine instead of chopping. Think about it.)

Grilled Steak and Vegetable Skewers with Chimichurri Sauce

Skewers assemble easily and help foods cook more quickly on the grill, so they're a great option for a weeknight meal. Argentinian Chimichurri Sauce—with fresh and dried herbs, garlic, red wine vinegar, and olive oil—brings out the best in almost any food. While the steak is marinating, make Packet Potatoes: Slice 4 unpeeled potatoes thinly into a large bowl, add 4 chopped green onions, 2 cloves of minced garlic, 2 tablespoons of olive oil, and salt and pepper to taste. Place the potato mixture on an 18-inch square sheet of heavy-duty foil and fold to make a foil packet (try to get the packet to the same overall thickness so it cooks evenly). Throw this packet on the grill about 15 minutes before the skewers. When you put the skewers on, turn the packet and cook for 10 minutes more. Open the packet at the table and spoon the potatoes onto each plate. Salute your efforts with a glass of Pinot Noir or Cabernet Sauvignon.

SERVES 4

> 1 pound boneless flank, hanger, or skirt steak
>
> 3 medium-size bell peppers in assorted colors (red, green, and yellow or orange), cored, seeded, and cut into wedges
>
> 1 large red onion, cut into 8 wedges
>
> 2 small yellow summer squash, ends trimmed and cut into 2-inch pieces

Chimichurri Sauce

MAKES ABOUT 1 CUP

> 1/4 cup chopped fresh Italian parsley leaves
>
> 1 teaspoon dried oregano
>
> 3 cloves garlic, minced
>
> 1/2 teaspoon red pepper flakes
>
> 1/2 teaspoon fine kosher or sea salt

$^1/_2$ **teaspoon freshly ground black pepper**

$^1/_2$ **cup olive oil**

$^1/_4$ **cup red wine vinegar**

12 wooden skewers, soaked in water for at least 30 minutes prior to grilling

1 Lay the steak on a cutting board so that the grain of the flesh is horizontal. Cut the steak lengthwise into 8 strips. Place the strips in a baking dish and set aside. Place the vegetables in a large zipper-top plastic bag.

2 Prepare a medium-hot fire in your grill.

3 In a medium-size bowl, whisk together the *Chimichurri Sauce* ingredients. Pour $^1/_3$ cup of the mixture over the steak, cover, and marinate for 15 minutes. Pour another $^1/_3$ cup over the vegetables in the bag, seal, toss to coat, and place on a baking sheet. Set the remaining mixture aside until ready to serve.

4 Thread the steak strips lengthwise onto 8 skewers. Discard the remaining steak marinade. Thread the vegetables onto the remaining 4 skewers, any way you want. Place the skewers on the baking sheet and take out to the grill.

5 Grill the vegetable skewers for 4 to 5 minutes per side, or until you have good grill marks. Grill the steak skewers, turning once with grill tongs, for 2 to 3 minutes per side for medium-rare or 4 to 5 minutes per side for medium. To serve, arrange the skewers on a platter and pass the remaining chimichurri sauce at the table.

Grilled Salt and Pepper–Style Rib-Eye Steak 'n' Onions with Orzo, Spinach, and Tomato Salad

Every once in a while, you need a dinner that's definitely man pleasin' without going the whole steak-and-potatoes route. This is it. If you're the queen in your family, give yourself the smaller-size steak and load up on the salad. Any leftover steak can be sliced up, mixed together with any leftover grilled and chopped onion, and added to the salad for the next day's lunch or a déjà vu dinner.

SERVES 4

Orzo, Spinach, and Tomato Salad

1 pound orzo, cooked according to package directions

1 pound baby spinach or larger-leafed spinach torn into small pieces

1 pint cherry or grape tomatoes, cut in half

1 cup (8 ounces) crumbled feta cheese

4 tablespoons olive oil

1 tablespoon fresh lemon juice

2 cloves garlic, minced

Fine kosher or sea salt and freshly ground black pepper to taste

2 large red onions, cut into ¹/₂-inch-thick slices

Four 6- to 8-ounce boneless rib-eye steaks, cut about ³/₄ inch thick

Olive oil for brushing

Coarse kosher or sea salt and cracked black peppercorns to taste

1 To make the *Orzo, Spinach, and Tomato Salad*, combine the orzo in a large serving bowl with the spinach, tomatoes, and feta. In a small bowl, whisk the olive oil, lemon juice, and garlic together. Season with salt and pepper, then pour over the salad and toss to blend. Set aside.

2   Prepare a hot fire in your grill. Oil a perforated grill rack.

3   Brush the onions, then the steaks, with olive oil and sprinkle with salt and pepper. Place on a doubled baking sheet to take out to the grill.

4   Place the onion slices on the prepared perforated grill rack and the steak directly on the grill rack. Grill the onion slices, turning once, for 6 to 10 minutes total, or until slightly charred and tender. Grill the steak, turning once, for 3 minutes per side for medium-rare or 4 minutes per side for medium. Transfer the cooked food to the clean baking sheet.

5   To serve, place the steaks on 4 dinner plates and top with the onion slices. Serve the salad on the side.

TIME-SAVING TIARA TOUCH

Make a big batch of orzo so that you can serve the rest as a side dish throughout the week. Just toss the cooked orzo with a little olive oil before storing it in the refrigerator in an airtight container.

Blackened Beef with Thai Chile Noodles, Mushrooms, and Baby Bok Choy

Now, this is a noodle bowl! And the leftovers for lunch the next day are fabulous, too. The flavors just keep getting better. That's the BBQ Queen way.

SERVES 4

Thai Chile Noodles

$^1/_4$ **cup olive oil**

1 tablespoon chile oil (optional)

$^1/_4$ **cup seasoned rice vinegar**

2 tablespoons chopped fresh mint leaves

2 tablespoons chopped fresh cilantro leaves

1 small chile pepper of your choice, seeded and minced

1 garlic clove, minced

8 ounces rice noodles or linguine, cooked according to package directions

$^1/_4$ **cup chopped, roasted peanuts**

2 teaspoons toasted sesame oil

2 tablespoons vegetable oil

4 large portobello mushrooms, stemmed

8 whole baby bok choy or 2 large heads bok choy cut into quarters

One 12-ounce, 1$^1/_2$-inch-thick boneless top sirloin or chuck steak

Fine kosher or sea salt and freshly ground black pepper to taste

1   To make the *Thai Chile Noodles*, combine the olive oil, chile oil, vinegar, herbs, chile, and garlic in a large bowl. Toss the cooked noodles with the dressing. Sprinkle on the peanuts and toss again. Set aside.

2   Prepare a hot fire in your grill.

3   Combine the sesame and vegetable oils in a small bowl. Brush the mushrooms and bok choy with this mixture, then the meat. Season all with salt and pepper. Place the steak and vegetables on a doubled baking sheet and take out to the grill.

4   Grill the steak for 3½ to 4 minutes per side for medium-rare or 5 minutes per side for medium. Grill the mushrooms and the bok choy for 2 to 3 minutes per side, turning once, or until you have good grill marks and the vegetables have begun to soften. Place the cooked food on the clean baking sheet and bring inside.

5   Slice the steak and mushrooms thinly. Place a serving of noodles in 4 bowls and top with the steak, mushrooms, and bok choy. Serve immediately.

Peppered Porterhouse with Stir-Grilled Vegetables

Instead of porterhouse, you could also grill rib-eye, T-bone, sirloin, or strip steak. (If you use a boneless steak, subtract about 1 minute from the total grilling time.) The simple punch of flavor from cracked peppercorns elevates this steak from the ordinary, and the vegetables are as easy to prepare as a visit to your local grocery store's salad bar. A glass of Merlot will complete this mighty fine meal. If you have leftovers, turn them into a peppery steak and vegetable soup by cutting the leftover steak and vegetables into small pieces and simmering them, with uncooked pasta if you like, in beef broth and a splash of red wine.

SERVES 4

2 tablespoons cracked black pepper

Three 1-pound porterhouse steaks, cut 1½ inches thick

2 cups cherry or grape tomatoes

2 cups chopped zucchini and yellow summer squash, mixed

1 cup chopped mixed red, green, and yellow bell peppers

1 cup chopped red onion

1 cup store-bought or homemade vinaigrette of your choice

Fine kosher or sea salt to taste

Extra virgin olive oil for drizzling

Freshly grated Parmesan cheese

You've Got Dinner!
MICRO-BAKED POTATOES

1 Prepare a hot fire in your grill. Oil all sides of a large grill wok.

2 Sprinkle the black pepper on the surface of the meat, pressing it in with your fingers. Place the vegetables in a zipper-top plastic bag and pour the vinaigrette over them. Seal the bag and toss to coat. Place a grill wok in the sink

and pour the vegetables into the grill wok, allowing them to drain. Place the grill wok and steaks on a doubled baking sheet and take out to the grill.

3   Place the grill wok on the grill first and grill the vegetables, tossing with wooden paddles or grill spatulas, until the tomatoes have split their skins, about 15 minutes. Grill the steaks on the grill grates for 5 minutes on each side for medium-rare or 6 minutes per side for medium. Transfer the cooked food to the clean baking sheet.

4   To serve, slice the steak thinly, arrange on 4 dinner plates, season with salt, and drizzle with olive oil. Serve with the vegetables topped with freshly grated Parmesan.

TIME-SAVING TIARA TOUCH

Diamonds are a girl's best friend, even at the grill. Make up a batch of Diamond Dust and keep it in a small glass jar in your cupboard, so it's ready to sprinkle on anything you want to grill. To make it, combine 2 tablespoons coarse kosher salt, 2 tablespoons garlic powder, and 1 tablespoon cracked black pepper.

Grilled Flank Steak with Avocado Salsa Verde and Grilled Corn

Big flavor, great color, and easy preparation are the hallmarks of a BBQ Queen's weeknight entrée, and this dish has them all. We just love it when a sauce can function as a vegetable, as it does here. Fresh tomatillos, those paper-husked small, green members of the tomato family, are available at larger supermarkets and Hispanic markets. If you can't get tomatillos in your area, substitute 2 cups of fresh chopped red tomato. You won't have salsa verde then, but it will still be durn good. If you wish, grill a second flank steak to have on hand for meals later in the week or for sandwiches.

SERVES 4

Avocado Salsa Verde

MAKES 2 CUPS

10 tomatillos, diced

$^1/_2$ cup chopped red onion

$^1/_4$ cup minced fresh cilantro

2 jalapeño peppers, seeded and minced

1 tablespoon fresh lime juice, or more to your taste

1 teaspoon fine kosher or sea salt

2 large ripe avocados

One 1$^1/_2$-pound flank steak

Olive oil for brushing

3 tablespoons fresh lime juice

Fine kosher or sea salt and freshly ground black pepper to taste

4 to 6 ears of corn, shucked

You've Got Dinner!
STEAMED RICE

1 Prepare a hot fire in your grill.

2 To make the *Avocado Salsa Verde*, combine the tomatillos, onion, cilantro, peppers, lime juice, and salt in a bowl. Peel and chop the avocados, add to the salsa, and stir to blend. Add more lime juice if necessary or desired. Cover and chill until ready to serve.

3 Rub the flank steak with olive oil and drizzle with some of the lime juice, then sprinkle with salt and pepper. Place in a zipper-top plastic bag or a disposable aluminum pan. Brush the corn with olive oil, then drizzle with lime juice and season with salt and pepper. Place the steak and corn on a doubled baking sheet to take out to the grill.

4 Grill the steak for about $2\frac{1}{2}$ to 3 minutes per side for medium-rare or 4 to 5 minutes per side for medium. Grill the corn, turning often, until the kernels have browned and softened, about 4 minutes total. Transfer the cooked food to the clean baking sheet.

5 Slice the steak on the diagonal, top the slices with the salsa, and accompany with the corn. Serve immediately.

Latin Lover's Carne Asada with Orange and Red Onion Mojo

When being a BBQ Queen starts to feel a little trying (all that waving, the glare of the tiaras, too much hot pink), we make this dish, guaranteed to restore some pep to your step. A mojo is a flavorful cross between a salsa and a sauce. More liquid than a salsa, less smooth than a sauce, mojos are good, good, good! We use this one as both a marinade and a finishing sauce. Included in this entrée are two servings of fruit (in the mojo and the grilled oranges) and one serving of vegetables. Since you're grilling whole heads of lettuce here, be sure to choose cylindrical heads (not the kinds with leaves flopping out all over the place). Reserve any leftover steak and mojo to top green salads or fill sandwiches later in the week. If you're really having a bad day, bring out margaritas made with pomegranate and lime juices to serve with this dish, or if that's too much trouble, a Jamaican Red Stripe beer.

SERVES 4

Orange and Red Onion Mojo

MAKES ABOUT 2 3/4 CUPS

1 cup orange juice

1/4 cup fresh lime juice (from about 4 limes)

1/2 cup finely chopped red onion

1 clove garlic, minced

3/4 cup olive oil

1/2 teaspoon dried oregano

Fine kosher or sea salt and freshly ground black pepper to taste

2 pounds beef skirt or flank steak, thinly cut

4 oranges, unpeeled and cut into 1/2-inch-thick slices

4 cylindrical heads of romaine lettuce

One 15-ounce can hearts of palm, chilled, drained, and chopped

You've Got Dinner!

STEAMED RICE, IF YOU WISH

1   To make the *Orange and Red Onion Mojo*, whisk together the orange and lime juices, onion, garlic, olive oil, oregano, salt, and pepper in a large bowl. Transfer half of this mixture to a zipper-top plastic bag. Add the steak, seal, toss, and let marinate at room temperature for 30 minutes. Reserve the remaining half of the mojo, covered, in the refrigerator.

2   Prepare a hot fire in your grill.

3   Place the steak, reserved mojo, sliced oranges, and romaine lettuce on a doubled baking sheet, along with a basting brush. Take out to the grill. Brush the orange slices and romaine with the mojo and grill, turning once, until slightly charred on all sides. Remove to the clean baking sheet.

4   Place the steak on the grill and grill, turning once, for 2 to 3 minutes per side for medium-rare or 3 to 4 minutes per side for medium. Discard the remaining steak marinade in the bag.

5   To serve, cut each head of romaine into bite-size pieces and arrange on each of 4 dinner plates with one-fourth of the hearts of palm. Serve the steak and orange slices on the side and drizzle all with the remaining reserved mojo.

TIME-SAVING TIARA TOUCH

Since the Orange and Red Onion Mojo is so versatile, make a double batch and refrigerate it in an airtight container. It's also great as a marinade for shrimp or halibut, as a dressing for a spinach salad, or even mixed into tuna salad.

Stir-Grilled Beef and Mushroom Marsala

Here's a grilled version of a trattoria classic. You can often buy Marsala, a sweet Italian fortified wine similar to sherry, in smaller bottles, so you don't have to splurge here. This dish comes together in less time than it takes a burning candle to drip down that Chianti bottle.

SERVES 4

Marsala Sauce
MAKES ABOUT ³/₄ CUP

¹/₄ cup **Marsala wine**

2 cloves **garlic, minced**

¹/₂ cup **olive oil**

2 tablespoons **finely chopped fresh Italian parsley**

Fresh lemon juice to taste

1 pound **beef tenderloin, cut into 1-inch pieces**

1¹/₂ cups **sliced button mushrooms**

1 pound **fettuccine, pappardelle, shells, or penne, cooked according to package directions**

¹/₂ cup **pasta cooking water**

You've Got Dinner!

BABY SPINACH SAUTÉED WITH OLIVE OIL AND GARLIC

1   In a small bowl, whisk together the *Marsala Sauce* ingredients. In a zipper-top plastic bag, pour in all but ¹/₃ cup of the sauce and add the beef pieces; set the reserved sauce aside. Seal the bag, toss to coat, refrigerate, and let marinate overnight, all day, or just while you heat the grill.

2   Prepare a hot fire in your grill. Spray a grill wok with cooking spray. Place the wok in the sink.

3   When ready to grill, add the mushrooms to the beef in the bag, seal, and shake a few times. Pour the beef, mushrooms, and their sauce into the grill wok and let drain. Place the grill wok on a doubled baking sheet and take out to the grill.

4 Stir-grill the beef and mushrooms, turning with wooden paddles or grill spatulas, until the beef is medium-rare, 10 to 12 minutes. Transfer to the clean baking sheet to bring inside. In a large bowl, toss the stir-grilled beef mixture with the hot pasta, adding the reserved Marsala sauce and enough pasta cooking water to moisten. Serve hot.

LIFE IN THE FAST LANE: KABOB-O-RAMA

Kabobs tend to be big family-pleasers, since they're fun both to look at and to eat. Remember, for best results, put the meat on separate kabobs from the vegetables so that you can get the timing right. You may use the homemade or store-bought marinades and rubs of your choice, or simply brush the kabobs with olive oil and season with salt, pepper, and herbs. Here are a few ideas:

- Kabobs of vinaigrette-marinated beef with kabobs of yellow summer squash chunks, zucchini chunks, and cherry tomatoes

- Kabobs of pork with kabobs of par-cooked sweet potato slices on rosemary skewers

- Kabobs of yellow curry–rubbed chicken with kabobs of par-cooked acorn or butternut squash cubes, red onion quarters, and apple slices

- Kabobs of shrimp with kabobs of fresh pineapple cubes, red pepper chunks, and red onion quarters

- Kabobs of pesto-basted scallops with kabobs of sugar snap peas and yellow or red teardrop tomatoes

- Kabobs of haloumi cheese chunks, cherry tomatoes, pitted green and black olives, and jarred peppadews

Tagliata with Greens

Tagliata, from the Italian *tagliare*, which means "to cut or carve," is a great week-night entrée that pays big benefits with delicious leftovers for salads or sand-wiches. The star is a 2-inch-thick boneless top sirloin steak, a cut that will weigh about 1½ pounds (so if you want more, go for 2 whole steaks). Serve slices of this rare steak on top of baby arugula, drizzle it with Balsamic Mustard Sauce, then garnish with shavings of Parmesan and wedges of lemon. It's heavenly.

Of course, you must have some Italian wine with this fine Italian dish. Since the Tuscans are known for their steak, pair this with a Tuscan red such as Sangiovese, Rosso di Montalcino, or a nice young Chianti.

SERVES 4

Balsamic Mustard Sauce
MAKES ABOUT ²/₃ CUP

¼ cup **Dijon mustard**

¼ cup **olive oil**

2 tablespoons **balsamic vinegar**

Fresh lemon juice to taste

You've Got Dinner!
GRILLED ITALIAN BREAD OR ASIAGO POLENTA (PAGE 36)

PLATTER OF SLICED TOMATOES

One 1½-pound **boneless sirloin steak, cut 2 inches thick**

3 tablespoons **olive oil**

3 large **cloves garlic, minced**

1 teaspoon **dried or 1 tablespoon fresh rosemary**

4 cups **baby arugula or spinach leaves (or other leafy lettuce of your choice)**

Lemon wedges for garnish

Small wedge (about 4 ounces) Parmesan cheese

1   Prepare a hot fire in your grill.

2   Whisk the *Balsamic Mustard Sauce* ingredients together in a small bowl. If you wish, funnel the sauce into a squeeze bottle or simply leave in the bowl, and set aside.

3   Place the steak on a doubled baking sheet. In a small bowl, mix the olive oil, garlic, and rosemary into a paste and spread over the surface of the meat.

4   Grill the steak for 8 minutes, turning once. Remove the steak from the grill and let the meat rest for 5 minutes on the clean baking sheet.

5   Place 1 cup of greens on each of 4 dinner plates. Slice the steak thinly and place the slices on top of the greens. Squeeze or drizzle the balsamic mustard sauce over the steak and greens and garnish each plate with lemon wedges. Pass the wedge of Parmesan, with a cheese parer or vegetable peeler, at the table and let diners shave their own cheese onto the tagliata.

Grilled Sirloin with Asparagus, Onions, and Gorgonzola Sauce

Some good bread to mop up the sauce, or a classic baked potato, is all you need to complete this meal. A 2-pound sirloin will also yield leftovers for future meals, another plus. The Gorgonzola Sauce is also delicious with grilled chicken or pork, burgers, or even drizzled over steamed vegetables.

SERVES 4

Gorgonzola Sauce
MAKES ABOUT 1 1/3 CUPS

1/2 cup (1 stick) unsalted butter, melted

1/4 cup Worcestershire sauce

3/4 cup (6 ounces) crumbled Gorgonzola or other blue cheese

1 clove garlic, minced

Fine kosher or sea salt and freshly ground black pepper to taste

One 1 1/2- to 2-pound boneless sirloin steak, cut 2 inches thick

3 tablespoons olive oil

3 large cloves garlic, minced

1 teaspoon dried or 1 tablespoon fresh rosemary

1 pound fresh asparagus, ends trimmed

2 large red onions, cut into 1-inch-thick slices

Olive oil for brushing

Fine kosher or sea salt and freshly ground black pepper to taste

You've Got Dinner!

ITALIAN BREAD OR BAKED POTATOES

1   Prepare a hot fire in your grill.

2   Whisk the *Gorgonzola Sauce* ingredients together in a small bowl and set aside.

3   Place the steak on a doubled baking sheet. Mix the olive oil, garlic, and rosemary into a paste and spread over the surface of the meat. Brush the asparagus spears and onion slices with olive oil and season with salt and pepper. Place on the sheet and carry everything out to the grill.

4   Place the onions on an oiled perforated grill rack and grill for 5 minutes per side. At the same time, grill the steak for 4 minutes per side, turning once. Remove the steak from the grill and let the meat rest for 5 minutes on the clean baking sheet. While the steak is resting, place the asparagus on the perforated grill rack and grill, turning often, until softened and browned, about 6 minutes.

5   To serve, slice the steak on the diagonal, nap with the sauce, and accompany with the asparagus and onion.

Martini-Marinated Filet Mignon with Sautéed Spinach and Pine Nuts

Vodka and vermouth are excellent in marinades for all kinds of meats and fish. We've chosen the quintessential filet mignon for a special weeknight supper. One of the great things about an expensive cut of beef is that the side dishes can be rather lowly and inexpensive. We like that! So get to work microwaving (or oven-baking) your baked potato. And here's a spinach recipe that cooks in only minutes. Horrors—you'll barely have time to sip a martini!

SERVES 4

Four 6- to 8-ounce filet mignons

2 teaspoons coarse kosher or sea salt

1 tablespoon coarsely ground black pepper

2 tablespoons finely chopped fresh parsley

2 tablespoons finely chopped chives

2 cloves garlic, minced

¹/₃ cup vodka

1 tablespoon dry vermouth

2 juniper berries

¹/₄ cup olive oil

You've Got Dinner!

ORZO, BAKED POTATOES, OR ROASTED POTATO WEDGES

Sautéed Spinach and Pine Nuts

2 tablespoons olive oil

3 tablespoons pine nuts

12 ounces baby spinach

1   Prepare a hot fire in your grill.

2   Rub the steaks with salt and pepper. Place the filets in a large zipper-top plastic bag and add the parsley, chives, garlic, vodka, vermouth, juniper

berries, and ¼ cup of the olive oil. Seal, toss to coat, and marinate in the refrigerator for 20 to 30 minutes.

3   In the meantime, get out a large sauté pan for the spinach. Have the 2 table-spoons of olive oil and pine nuts close by. (You'll sauté the spinach as soon as the steaks are pulled from the grill, which gives it a couple of minutes to rest.)

4   Remove the steaks from the marinade, discarding the marinade, and grill the steaks, covered, for 3 minutes on each side for medium-rare or 4 min-utes on each side for medium. Place on a platter.

5   To make the *Sautéed Spinach and Pine Nuts*, heat the olive oil over medium-high heat in the sauté pan. Add the pine nuts and cook for 1 to 2 minutes to brown lightly. Remove the nuts from the pan. Add the spinach and toss to coat all of the spinach lightly and heat through, 3 to 4 minutes. Sprinkle the pine nuts on top.

6   Serve the steaks immediately, with the sautéed spinach on the side.

TIME-SAVING TIARA TOUCH

Baby spinach is often sold in 6-ounce bags in the market, so if you find them you can grab two and go, rather than scooping and weighing loose spinach leaves.

Stir-Grilled Spaghetti with Meat Sauce and a Kiss of Smoke

No, you're not reading this wrong. You really can do spaghetti on the grill—to a point. When Judith was in Girl Scouts, back in the Dark Ages, she used to make coffee-can suppers over the campfire and wondered why the mixture of ground beef, onions, and spaghetti with meat sauce didn't taste the same when cooked on the stove at home. (Ah, yes, even then she loved to eat well.) The reason? Wood smoke flavoring. Here, you can have that flavor (without actually camping out, unless you want to) in your own backyard. On a gas grill, use a foil packet with holes poked through the top to enclose 1 cup of dry wood chips or $1/3$ cup dry wood pellets. On a charcoal grill, add moistened wood chips or a foil packet containing dry wood pellets directly to the coals after the fire is hot.

SERVES 4

One 1-pound package spaghetti, cooked according to package directions

One 16-ounce jar spaghetti sauce of your choice

1 pound ground beef

1 medium-size onion, chopped

Fine kosher or sea salt and freshly ground black pepper to taste

1 cup wood chips or $1/3$ cup wood pellets (see above)

Freshly grated Romano or Parmesan cheese to taste

You've Got Dinner!

GRILLED GARLIC BREAD

GREEN SALAD

1   Prepare a hot fire in your grill. For a gas grill, immediately place the packet of dry chips or pellets on the grill grate toward the back of the grill and close the lid. The chips will begin to smoke after 20 minutes. For a charcoal fire, sprinkle moistened wood chips or place a foil packet containing dry wood pellets on the hot coals right before grilling. Oil both sides of a large grill wok and place on the grill.

2 In a large bowl, toss the cooked pasta with half of the spaghetti sauce, reserving the remaining half. Combine the ground beef, onion, salt, and pepper in a large zipper-top plastic bag. Place both on a baking sheet to take out to the grill.

3 When the fire is hot, place the meat mixture in the prepared grill wok. Stir-grill, turning with wooden paddles or grill spatulas, with the grill lid closed as much as possible, until the beef has browned, 15 to 20 minutes. Add the spaghetti and toss over the direct fire for about 4 to 5 minutes. Move the wok to the indirect side of the grill and close the lid. Let smoke for about 10 minutes, opening the lid and tossing every 2 to 3 minutes. Transfer the wok to the baking sheet.

4 Spoon the spaghetti into 4 pasta bowls and add some of the reserved spaghetti sauce to each bowl. Top with freshly grated cheese and serve immediately.

Pig Out

Pork is another great option for busy weeknight grilling. Go for already tender cuts such as thin- to thick-cut pork chops, pork tenderloin, or center-cut pork fillet, as well as sausages of all kinds and ham.

In many of the recipes in this chapter, we've added a touch of sweet-ness with jams, honey, cider, brown sugar, or fresh fruits to bring out the essentially sweet flavor of the pork. In other recipes, we offer a flavor contrast of spice or heat or simple savoriness.

The BBQ Queens love cuts of pork simply grilled (is there anything better than a juicy, perfectly grilled pork chop or pork tenderloin?), but also jazzed up a little bit. Try stir-grilling pieces of ham or sausage with endive or kale, along with potatoes, for a new and time-saving take on a traditionally slow-simmered dish. Thread pieces of pork tenderloin onto skewers, then baste with a rum-enhanced mixture. Or place medallions of pork in a foil packet along with sweet potatoes, bananas, and a Caribbean-style butter.

Coriander-Crusted
Thick Pork Chops with
Stir-Grilled Red Onions
and Apples   122

Grilled Pork Chops
with Squash, Apples, and
Cider-Bourbon Jus   124

Rum-Basted Pork
Tenderloin on
Sugar Cane Skewers
with Grilled Mango
and Pineapple Salsa   126

Grilled Pork Tenderloin
with Chive-Buttered
Corn on the Cob   128

Caribbean Grilled Pork
Tenderloin Packets with
Rum-Glazed Sweet
Potatoes and Bananas   130

Tandoori-Rubbed Pork
Tenderloin with Stir-Grilled
Coconut Beans   132

Sesame Spice–Rubbed
Pork Tenderloin with
Orange-Fennel Salad   134

Stir-Grilled
Moo Shu Pork   136

Grilled Sausage, Artichoke,
and Chickpea Soup   138

Stir-Grilled Sausage,
Endive, and
Baby Potatoes   140

Wham-Bam Ham with
Apricot Jam Glaze and
Cheesy Horseradish
Potatoes   142

We'll have you out to the grill and back inside again—fast! And with left-over grilled goodies, you'll prop up your feet and enjoy a glass of wine another night, while dinner is basically done.

Coriander-Crusted Thick Pork Chops with Stir-Grilled Red Onions and Apples

Thick-cut bone-in pork chops take twice as long on the grill as boneless butter-flied chops, but they are worth the extra time because they are oh, so good. The coating of Dijon mustard helps keep the chop moist during cooking, plus it adds lots of flavor. The stir-grilled apples and onions are a takeoff on the traditional Southern casserole. We've added honey to finish them off since they aren't simmering in their own juices.

SERVES 4

Four 6- to 8-ounce bone-in pork chops, 1 1/2 inches thick

3 tablespoons Dijon mustard

2 tablespoons ground coriander

1 teaspoon ground cumin

3 medium-size crisp apples, such as Granny Smith or Jonathan, peeled, cored, and cut into 3/4-inch-thick slices

1 large red onion, sliced into 1/2-inch wedges

Kosher or sea salt and freshly ground black pepper to taste

2 tablespoons amber honey, such as clover or wildflower

You've Got Dinner!

BISCUITS WITH BUTTER AND HONEY

GREEN SALAD OR THREE-BEAN SALAD

1   Rinse the pork chops and pat dry. Place on a doubled baking sheet. In a small bowl, combine the mustard, coriander, and cumin, stirring to blend. Slather the mixture on the pork chops and set aside.

2   Prepare a medium fire in your grill.

3   Oil a grill wok on both sides and place the apple and onion slices in the wok. Season with salt and pepper and set on the baking sheet to take out to the grill.

4   At the grill, start the pork chops first. Grill on one side for about 15 minutes, then turn to finish cooking, about another 15 minutes.

5   After the pork chops have been on the grill for 10 minutes, place the wok filled with the apples and onions on the grill. Toss the apples and onions several times during the cooking until they have softened, 15 to 20 minutes. Transfer the pork and the wok to the clean baking sheet.

6   Set a pork chop on each of 4 dinner plates and add one-fourth of the apples and onions. Drizzle each portion with $1/2$ tablespoon of honey and serve.

LIFE IN THE FAST LANE: SPRINKLES

 Like magic fairy dust, spice sprinkles can bring your food to life. We especially like spices that do double duty, such as hickory salt, pepper blends, powdered Worcestershire, Beau Monde seasoning, and other seasoning mixtures. Sprinkle on vegetables, pork, poultry, wild game, beef, fish, and shellfish. Here are simple ways to cast your weeknight grilling spell:

- **Hickory salt and seasoned pepper**

- **Powdered Worcestershire and ground white pepper**

- **Ground chipotle pepper and celery salt**

- **Beau Monde seasoning and ground black and green peppercorns**

- **Chinese five-spice powder and sea salt**

- **Garlic or onion salt and lemon pepper**

Grilled Pork Chops with Squash, Apples, and Cider-Bourbon Jus

The flavors in this dish go together so well that everyone at the table will belong to the Clean Plate Club. To give us time to freshen up our makeup before dinner, we like to micro-cook the squash until it's almost done, then give it a little char on the grill to finish. Golden Delicious apples work great for quick grilling because they're naturally sweeter and softer than Jonathan and Granny Smith apples. Try this dish with a glass of cold cider (sparkling or still).

SERVES 4

Cider-Bourbon Jus
MAKES ABOUT 1 CUP

1 cup apple cider or apple juice

2 tablespoons unsalted butter

1 tablespoon bourbon or rum

Salt and freshly ground white pepper to taste

2 acorn squash, halved horizontally, seeds removed, and micro-cooked on high for 8 minutes

Kosher or sea salt and freshly ground white pepper to taste

4 Golden Delicious apples, tops and bottoms trimmed off

4 boneless pork loin chops, cut ³/₄ inch thick

1 To make the *Cider-Bourbon Jus*, bring the cider to a boil over high heat in a small saucepan. Boil for 10 to 15 minutes, or until it has reduced to ¹/₂ cup. Remove from the heat and whisk in the butter and bourbon. Season with salt and pepper. Transfer ¹/₃ cup to a small ramekin and set the remaining jus aside.

2 Prepare a hot fire in your grill. Oil a perforated grill rack and have it ready by the grill.

3   Slice the partially cooked squash into ³/₄-inch rings and place on a baking sheet. Brush each ring with a little of the jus from the ramekin, season with salt and pepper, and arrange into stacks. Slice each apple horizontally into 4 slices, then use a paring knife to remove the core in each slice. Place the apple rings on the baking sheet and brush each with a little of the jus. On a separate baking sheet, place the pork chops and brush both sides with the last of the jus in the ramekin. Sprinkle each chop with salt and pepper.

4   At the grill, place the apple rings on the prepared perforated grill rack. Place the grill rack on the grill, close the lid, and grill for 2 to 3 minutes. Turn the apple slices with grill tongs, close the lid, and grill for 2 to 3 minutes more, or until the apple rings have grill marks and they "give" when gently squeezed with the tongs. Transfer the apple rings back to their baking sheet and place the squash rings on the grill rack. Close the lid and grill for 4 minutes, then turn and grill for 3 to 4 minutes more, or until the squash rings have grill marks and are cooked through. Transfer back to their baking sheet. Remove the perforated grill rack. Place the pork chops on the grill and grill for 7¹/₂ minutes total, turning once.

5   Arrange the squash and apple rings around the edges of a large serving platter, place the pork in the middle, and drizzle everything with the reserved jus. Serve immediately.

Rum-Basted Pork Tenderloin on Sugar Cane Skewers with Grilled Mango and Pineapple Salsa

If you love Caribbean rum drinks, you'll love the flavor that this marinade imparts to the pork tenderloin on the grill. If you can find stalks of fresh sugar cane, which are available in Latin and Asian groceries, they add a certain island flair to this dish.

SERVES 4

Caribbean Baste

MAKES ABOUT 1 $^1/_4$ CUPS

You've Got Dinner!

STEAMED RICE, IF YOU WISH

> $^1/_3$ **cup light rum**
>
> $^1/_3$ **cup fresh lime juice (from about 5 or 6 limes)**
>
> $^1/_2$ **cup olive oil**
>
> **2 cloves garlic, minced**
>
> **1 tablespoon minced shallot**
>
> **Fine kosher or sea salt and freshly ground black pepper to taste**

> **1 $^1/_2$ pounds pork tenderloin, cut into 1-inch chunks**
>
> **1 mango, peeled, pitted, and cut into wedges**
>
> **1 small pineapple, peeled, cored, and cut into 1-inch-thick rings**
>
> **1 large red onion, cut into 1-inch-thick slices**
>
> **8 slender stalks of fresh sugar cane or 8 wooden skewers, soaked in water for at least 30 minutes before grilling**
>
> $^1/_2$ **cup chopped fresh cilantro leaves**
>
> **1 jalapeño or small red chile pepper, seeded and minced**

1   Combine the *Caribbean Baste* ingredients in a small bowl. Place the pork tenderloin in a large zipper-top plastic bag and pour in $^1/_2$ cup of the baste. Place the mango, pineapple, and onion in a second zipper-top plastic bag

and pour ¼ cup of the reserved baste over them. Seal and toss both bags to coat the pork and fruits with the baste. Set aside for 15 minutes. Reserve the remaining baste and set aside.

2   Prepare a medium-hot fire in your grill. Oil a perforated grill rack and place it by the grill.

3   Remove the pork from the marinade and thread onto the sugar cane stalks. Do not crowd the pork. Place the pork skewers and the bag of fruits on a doubled baking sheet and take out to the grill.

4   Place the skewers on the grill grate. Remove the fruits and onion from the bag with a slotted spoon and place them on the prepared perforated grill rack. Cover and grill for 4 to 5 minutes. When the pork has turned opaque on the bottom, turn the skewers. Turn the fruits and onion. Cover and cook for another 3 to 4 minutes, or until the pork is opaque and firm all the way through. Transfer to the clean baking sheet.

5   To serve, place 2 skewers on each of 4 plates. Coarsely chop the grilled mango, pineapple, and onion and place in a large bowl. Add the cilantro and jalapeño. Pour over the reserved remaining baste, toss to blend, and serve with the skewers.

TIME-SAVING TIARA TOUCH

You can find fresh pineapple that has already been peeled and cored in the produce section of your grocery store.

Grilled Pork Tenderloin with Chive-Buttered Corn on the Cob

Our Coarse BBQ Rub makes a nice crust on the tenderloin. The Chive Butter is delicious on the corn and can do double duty served with bread or melted on an additional steamed vegetable of your choice, such as carrots or peas. The pork and corn grill at the same time and take up most of the grill surface, so add sides that don't need to be grilled. If you want some heat, add a shake of red pepper flakes or a teaspoon or so of finely chopped jalapeño pepper.

SERVES 4

BBQ Queens' Coarse BBQ Rub

MAKES ABOUT I CUP

^{1}/$_4$ cup coarse black pepper

^{1}/$_4$ cup sweet paprika

2 tablespoons granulated garlic

I tablespoon dry mustard

I tablespoon whole celery seed

I tablespoon dark brown sugar

2 teaspoons coarse kosher or sea salt

You've Got Dinner!

POTATO SALAD

CHOPPED PINEAPPLE MIXED WITH CHOPPED RED ONION AND LIME JUICE

Chive Butter

MAKES ABOUT ^{3}/$_4$ CUP

^{1}/$_2$ cup (I stick) unsalted butter, softened

^{1}/$_4$ cup snipped chives (or other fresh herbs of your choice)

Two I-pound pork tenderloins

2 tablespoons olive oil

4 ears corn

1 Combine the **BBQ Queens' Coarse BBQ Rub** ingredients in a glass jar with a tight-fitting lid. Shake to blend.

2 Combine the **Chive Butter** ingredients in a small bowl.

3 Prepare a hot fire in your grill.

4 In a glass baking dish, coat the tenderloins with oil and sprinkle 2 or 3 tablespoons of the rub on each tenderloin.

5 Pull back the husks from each ear of corn and remove the corn silks. Pull half of the husks back over the corn and brush each ear with 1 tablespoon of the chive butter. Close the husks. Put everything on a baking sheet to take out to the grill.

6 Grill the tenderloins and corn, turning several times, for 15 to 20 minutes. The corn may be done after 10 minutes, so watch it. The internal temperature of the tenderloin should be about 140°F for medium-rare and 150°F for medium. Let the meat stand for 5 minutes, then slice and serve with the corn and other sides of your choice.

Caribbean Grilled Pork Tenderloin Packets with Rum-Glazed Sweet Potatoes and Bananas

When you open this foil packet, hot from the grill, the aroma is heavenly! You can prepare the packets and refrigerate them for up to 1 day ahead of time if you wish. Because of the sugar in the packets, it's best to use a medium fire so everything cooks, but doesn't turn to carbon. If you have an aversion to canned sweet potatoes, get over it! They taste great and make this recipe super easy.

SERVES 4

$1^3/_4$ **pounds pork tenderloin or center-cut pork fillet, cut into $^1/_2$-inch-thick medallions**

Two 15-ounce cans sliced sweet potatoes, drained

2 large bananas, peeled and sliced into rounds

1 large red onion, sliced into rings

$^1/_4$ cup ($^1/_2$ stick) unsalted butter

4 tablespoons packed light brown sugar

4 tablespoons light, dark, or spiced rum (optional)

Fine kosher or sea salt and freshly ground white pepper to taste

1   Prepare a medium fire in your grill.

2   Take four 18 x 18-inch sheets of heavy-duty aluminum foil, lay each sheet on a flat surface, and spray with cooking spray. Divide the pork medallions among the foil sheets, arranging them in one layer. Divide the sweet potato, banana, and red onion slices among the foil sheets.

3   In a small bowl, mix together the butter, brown sugar, rum, if using, and salt and pepper. Place a dollop of this mixture on top of the pork. Wrap and seal the foil to form 4 packets.

4   Grill, seam side up, with the grill lid down, for 25 minutes. Do not turn. To serve, place a packet on each plate, let cool slightly, then open. Transfer the contents to the plate and discard the foil.

LIFE IN THE FAST LANE: SAUCES IN A FLASH

 Begin with good-quality mayonnaise and add to it. How easy is that? Ingredients for doctoring up your own sauce include pesto, sun-dried tomatoes, olives, citrus, red peppers, onions, fresh herbs, and horseradish.

Roasted Red Pepper Sauce: In a food processor, place 1 cup mayonnaise, 1 cup roasted red peppers from a jar, and 2 tablespoons lemon juice. Process until smooth. Season to taste with kosher salt and seasoned pepper. This sauce is versatile enough to serve with just about any grilled meat or seafood.

Pesto Sauce: In a food processor, place 1 cup mayonnaise and $1/3$ cup prepared pesto. Process until smooth. Season to taste with kosher salt and seasoned pepper. Serve with poultry, fish, shellfish, or vegetables.

Kalamata Olive and Orange Sauce: In a food processor, place 1 cup mayonnaise, $1/2$ cup pitted Kalamata olives, and the zest and juice of 1 orange. Process until smooth. Season to taste with kosher salt and seasoned pepper. Serve with fish, shellfish, chicken, or beef.

Chipotle and Cilantro Sauce: In a food processor, place 1 cup mayonnaise, 1 chipotle pepper from a can of chipotles in adobo sauce, the zest and juice of 1 lime, and 2 tablespoons snipped cilantro. Process until smooth. Season to taste with kosher salt and seasoned pepper. This sauce is especially good with pork, chicken, turkey, or shrimp.

Tandoori-Rubbed Pork Tenderloin with Stir-Grilled Coconut Beans

This fragrant, spicy, and grainy rub creates a crisp outer crust on the tenderloin that's very nice. The stir-grilled green beans have just a hint of unsweetened coconut (look in your local health food store) and the same spice mixture. Ginger-spiced iced tea rounds out the Indian theme.

SERVES 4 TO 6

Tandoori Rub

MAKES ABOUT ³/₄ CUP

I tablespoon ground ginger

I tablespoon ground cumin

I tablespoon ground coriander

I tablespoon ground paprika

I tablespoon turmeric

I tablespoon cayenne pepper

¹/₂ tablespoon coarse kosher or sea salt

Two I¹/₂-pound pork tenderloins

I tablespoon olive oil, plus more for drizzling

I pound green beans, ends trimmed

I tablespoon unsweetened dried coconut

You've Got Dinner!

ONION, TOMATO, AND CUCUMBER RAITA (PAGE 90)

1 Prepare a hot fire in your grill.

2 Combine the *Tandoori Rub* ingredients in a small bowl and whisk to blend.

3 On a doubled baking sheet, coat the tenderloins with 1 tablespoon of the olive oil and sprinkle with all but 1 tablespoon of the rub. In a large bowl, drizzle the beans with olive oil, sprinkle with the remaining 1 tablespoon of rub and the coconut, and toss to blend. Oil both sides of a perforated grill

wok and transfer the bean mixture to the grill wok. Place the wok on the doubled baking sheet.

4   Grill the tenderloins for 15 to 20 minutes, turning every 5 minutes, or until the internal temperature of the meat is 140° to 145°F for rare or 150°F for medium. At the same time, grill the beans in the grill wok, tossing with wooden paddles or grill spatulas, until they are crisp-tender, 15 to 20 minutes. Transfer the cooked food to the clean baking sheet. Let the pork stand for 5 minutes, then slice and serve with the beans alongside.

TIME-SAVING TIARA TOUCH

The Tandoori Rub will keep for months in an airtight container, so why not make extra to try on chicken, turkey, or swordfish?

Sesame Spice–Rubbed Pork Tenderloin with Orange-Fennel Salad

The flavor of orange infuses this meal, adding sweetness to balance the hot ingredients in the rub. And the orange contrasts beautifully with the slight bitterness of the fennel. The Sesame Spice Rub, which will keep for several weeks in an airtight container, is also good on chicken.

SERVES 4

2 pounds pork tenderloin

2 tablespoons olive oil

2 large fennel bulbs, ends and feathery tops trimmed

2 large oranges, peeled and segmented

Zest and juice of 1 lemon

6 tablespoons extra virgin olive oil

Coarse kosher or sea salt and freshly ground black pepper to taste

2 ounces Asiago cheese, freshly shaved, for garnish

Sesame Spice Rub

MAKES 1 CUP

1/2 cup sesame seeds

3 tablespoons dried orange peel

2 tablespoons ground ginger

1 tablespoon garlic salt

1 tablespoon ground anise

1 tablespoon red pepper flakes

You've Got Dinner!

STEAMED SPINACH OR BROCCOLI

ORZO OR STEAMED RICE, IF YOU WISH

1 Prepare a medium-hot fire in your grill.

2 Place the pork on a doubled baking sheet. Lightly brush both sides of the pork with the 2 tablespoons olive oil and season with salt and pepper. Set aside.

3 Thinly slice the fennel and place in a large bowl with the orange segments. Combine the lemon zest and juice with the extra virgin olive oil and stir to blend. Pour about 4 tablespoons of the lemon mixture over the fennel salad. Reserve the rest of the lemon–olive oil mixture to drizzle over the grilled pork.

4 Combine the *Sesame Spice Rub* ingredients in a small bowl. Stir to blend. Sprinkle 2 to 3 tablespoons of the mixture over the tenderloin.

5 Grill the pork for about 10 minutes per side, until an instant-read thermometer registers 145°F.

6 Let the pork rest for 3 to 4 minutes, then slice into 1-inch-thick slices. Place an equal amount of slices on each of 4 dinner plates and drizzle with the remaining lemon–olive oil mixture. Add a serving of the fennel salad topped with shavings of Asiago cheese.

Stir-Grilled Moo Shu Pork

In this fresh spin on a Chinese takeout classic, you get a fusion of flavors from the grill and the Asian ingredients. If you want, you can substitute fresh lettuce leaves to use as "cups" or wraps for the filling instead of the flour tortillas.

SERVES 4

1 pound pork tenderloin, cut into cubes

2 cloves garlic, minced

¼ cup low-sodium soy sauce

2 tablespoons rice vinegar

2 teaspoons toasted sesame oil

15 green onions, sliced (white and green parts)

2 teaspoons grated fresh ginger

4 cups finely shredded cabbage

One 8-ounce can sliced water chestnuts, drained

8 large flour tortillas

Vegetable oil for brushing

Store-bought hoisin or plum sauce of your choice

You've Got Dinner!
STEAMED BROCCOLI

1   Prepare a hot fire in your grill.

2   In a large bowl, combine the pork, garlic, soy sauce, vinegar, sesame oil, green onions, and ginger until well blended. Stir in the cabbage and water chestnuts. Spray the inside of a perforated grill wok with cooking spray and place on a doubled baking sheet. Brush the tortillas on both sides with vegetable oil and place on the baking sheet.

3   Spoon the pork mixture into the grill wok and take outside. Place the grill wok directly on the grill grate. Stir-grill for 20 to 25 minutes, turning the pork and vegetables with grill spatulas or wooden paddles every 1 to 2 minutes, until the pork has browned and the vegetables have softened and browned. Grill the tortillas for 2 minutes, turning once, until grill marks appear on both sides. Remove the cooked food to the clean baking sheet.

4 Serve family-style by placing the pork mixture on a large serving platter. Let each diner spoon pork into the middle of a flour tortilla, dollop with sauce, and roll up.

TIME-SAVING TIARA TOUCH

Include good-quality Asian ingredients like hoisin or plum sauce, canned water chestnuts, and toasted sesame oil in your pantry. Refrigerate hoisin or plum sauce after you open it.

Grilled Sausage, Artichoke, and Chickpea Soup

Char-grill a passel of sausages. Have some for dinner one night with sautéed peppers and onions, and save the leftovers for this crowd-pleasing soup, which comes together in a snap. Shop for wonderful boutique Italian sausages at better grocery stores such as Whole Foods Market. Or select from a vast array of sausages at an Italian market or a German butcher shop.

SERVES 6

I pound leftover grilled pork (or chicken) sausage

I large red onion, chopped

One 15-ounce can chickpeas, drained

One 14-ounce can artichoke hearts, drained, or one 9-ounce package frozen artichoke hearts, thawed

One 28-ounce can Italian plum tomatoes with their juice

3 cups store-bought or homemade chicken broth

I teaspoon dried oregano

I teaspoon dried basil

I teaspoon fennel seed

¼ pound orzo (optional)

Fine kosher or sea salt and freshly ground black pepper to taste

1   Slice the grilled sausage into bite-size pieces. Place the sausage pieces, red onion, and chickpeas in a large soup pot over medium heat.

2   Cut the artichoke hearts and the tomatoes into bite-size pieces and add them to the pot. Pour in the chicken stock, then add the oregano, basil, and fennel.

3   Bring to a boil, then reduce the heat to low and simmer, uncovered, for 30 minutes. If using the orzo, add it and cook for an additional 15 minutes, until the pasta is *al dente*. Season with salt and pepper and serve.

With a simple grilled entrée, a chutney can be divine. Part sweet, part savory, a chutney is 100 percent delicious. Chutneys go especially well with spicy foods like blackened or zesty barbecue-rubbed foods and are versatile enough to use as a side condiment or as a spread for sandwiches. And what's even better, they can be simple to make. Start with a good-quality jam or seedless preserves. Then add chopped fruit, vegetables, and seasoning. *Voilà!*

Orange and Red Onion Chutney: Stir together 1 cup orange marmalade, $^1/_2$ cup chopped red onion, $^1/_2$ cup snipped dried apricots, and ground white pepper and kosher salt to taste. Try this on poultry, pork, or meaty fish such as swordfish or halibut.

Raspberry Jalapeño Chutney: Stir together 1 cup seedless raspberry preserves, $^1/_2$ cup finely chopped jalapeño, $^1/_2$ cup chopped green onion, 2 teaspoons lime/lemon zest, and lime/lemon juice to taste. This is delicious with grilled pork or duck.

Plum Chutney: Stir together 1 cup plum jam or preserves, $^1/_2$ cup dried cranberries, $^1/_2$ cup chopped green onion, 1 tablespoon freshly grated ginger, and kosher salt to taste. This goes great with beef or turkey.

Apricot Chutney: Stir together 1 cup apricot preserves, $^1/_4$ cup snipped dried apples, $^1/_4$ cup golden raisins, lemon zest and juice to taste, and red pepper flakes to taste. Serve this chutney with poultry or pork.

Stir-Grilled Sausage, Endive, and Baby Potatoes

One December evening, Judith was standing out at the grill in the midst of making this dish for dinner. She noticed how nice it was to stand somewhere warm and look up at the starry night sky. That's being in the moment, or whatever. This dish, a grilled reconstruction of the classic ham-wrapped endive topped with cheese sauce, is great to serve on a chilly night. Just remember to close the grill lid between stirs, so that you keep in maximum heat. For ease in serving, just turn the contents of the grill wok onto a large serving platter and top with the grated cheese.

SERVES 4

1 pound new potatoes

1 large red onion, cut into 8 wedges

6 Belgian endives (also known as chicory or witloof chicory), ends trimmed and cut lengthwise into quarters

1 pound smoked sausage or ham steak, cut into bite-size pieces

Olive oil for drizzling

Kosher or sea salt and freshly ground black pepper to taste

Emmental or Gruyère cheese, shredded, for garnish

You've Got Dinner!

GREEN SALAD WITH A LEMONY VINAIGRETTE

1 Prepare a hot fire in your grill.

2 While the grill is heating, prick the potatoes all over with a paring knife or fork. Microwave on high for 6 to 7 minutes, or until they can easily be pierced with a paring knife or fork. Cut them into quarters.

3 Place the potatoes, onion, endives, and sausage in a large bowl, drizzle with olive oil, and toss to coat. Season with salt and pepper and toss again. Oil

both sides of a perforated grill wok, place on a baking sheet, and turn the mixture out into the grill wok. Take the tray out to the grill.

4   Place the grill wok directly on the grill grate. Stir-grill for 20 to 25 minutes, turning the mixture with grill spatulas or wooden paddles every 1 to 2 minutes, until the potatoes, onion, endive, and sausage have softened and browned. Arrange the vegetables and sausage on a platter and sprinkle with the shredded cheese. Serve immediately.

TIME-SAVING TIARA TOUCH

Grill extra sausage to use later in the week to make Grilled Sausage, Artichoke, and Chickpea Soup (page 138) even easier.

Wham-Bam Ham with Apricot Jam Glaze and Cheesy Horseradish Potatoes

This tasty meal from the grill is super quick because the ham is already cooked. You simply give it a bit of char and heat it through. Hurry the potatoes by pre-cooking them in the microwave, and also choose a simple side vegetable that can be cooked while the potatoes are in the microwave. Sweet and savory Apricot Jam Glaze does double duty as a glaze on the meat and as a bread spread. Apply the glaze to the ham during the last 3 to 4 minutes of cooking to avoid burning the sugar.

SERVES 4

Four ¹/₂-inch-thick precooked ham slices

Apricot Jam Glaze
MAKES ABOUT 1 ¹/₄ CUPS

¹/₂ **cup apricot jam or preserves**

¹/₄ **cup (¹/₂ stick) unsalted butter, melted**

2 tablespoons fresh lemon juice

2 tablespoons dry mustard

2 tablespoons orange zest

1 teaspoon red pepper flakes

You've Got Dinner!
STEAMED GREEN BEANS, ASPARAGUS, OR BROCCOLI

Cheesy Horseradish Potatoes

4 medium-size red potatoes, sliced ¹/₄ inch thick

6 tablespoons whipping cream

3 tablespoons fresh horseradish

Kosher or sea salt and freshly ground black pepper to taste

6 tablespoons shredded cheddar cheese

1   Place the ham slices on a platter. Prepare a hot fire in your grill.

2   To make the *Apricot Jam Glaze*, combine the apricot jam and the butter in a small saucepan, cooking over low heat until liquefied. Add the lemon juice, dry mustard, orange zest, and red pepper flakes, stirring to combine. Remove from the heat and set aside.

3   To make the *Cheesy Horseradish Potatoes*, precook the potato slices in the microwave for about 2 minutes or until tender when pierced with a fork. Remove from the microwave and arrange the potato slices in an 8-inch-square disposable aluminum pan. In a small bowl, combine the whipping cream and horseradish and pour over the potatoes. Sprinkle with salt and pepper. Top with the cheddar cheese and cover the pan with a piece of aluminum foil. Place the pan over the fire on the grill and cook for 7 to 8 minutes.

4   Place the ham slices on the grill and cook for 2 minutes per side. Then baste both sides with the glaze and cook another 1 to 2 minutes per side.

5   Serve the ham slices with the remaining glaze on the side and a portion of the potatoes.

Hen Party

In most American homes, what's sizzling on the grill on a weeknight is probably something in the poultry family. Not that we don't love our burgers and steaks, hot dogs and sausages—it's just that boneless chicken and turkey have so much going for them.

Boneless, skinless chicken breast is now available at grocery stores everywhere. It's fast, convenient, and healthy. The only problem is how to grill it so that it gets done evenly. Here's where the BBQ Queens come to the rescue with the "paillard," a French term for a piece of poultry or meat pounded to an even thickness. Use the edge of a sturdy saucer or a meat mallet to pound the chicken breast to about a $1/2$-inch thickness. Over a hot fire, your paillard will take exactly 5 minutes of total grilling time. It doesn't get any easier—and more delicious—than that!

Turkey is also fast becoming a popular dinnertime option. You don't have to roast the whole bird anymore, since there are now turkey breast tenderloins and cutlets in addition to the ground turkey available at the grocery store. Because turkey has a little less moisture than chicken, we recommend grilling it over a medium-hot fire, not a hot

one. A quick brush of olive oil or an easy marinade also helps keep turkey moist as it cooks. Both turkey and chicken are done when a meat thermometer inserted into the thickest part registers 165°F. For safety's sake, some people will tell you to grill poultry to 170°F or even 180°F. We like to grill ours a little less, to 160° to 165°F, because the chicken or turkey keeps cooking after you pull it off the grill. So cooking it to 165°F means that by the time it is served, it will increase at least another 5 degrees to 170°F. The BBQ Queens also agree that once you overcook your food, there is nothing you can do about it.

Tunisian-Spiced Flattened Chicken Breasts

Wonderful and fragrant aromas will permeate the backyard when you grill this delicious chicken dish. The preparation we've provided is simple and good, with an embellished couscous that tastes great with whatever dried fruits you have to add to it, even if it's just raisins. Drizzle red onion slices with the olive oil and lemon mixture and grill them alongside the chicken. Pile the couscous in the center of the platter, place the grilled chicken on top of it, and surround with the caramelized onion slices. This is great with a medium-dark ale or sweet iced tea.

SERVES 4

Tunisian Grilling Spice Mixture
MAKES ABOUT $1/4$ CUP

I tablespoon ground cumin

I tablespoon sweet paprika

I tablespoon ground coriander

I teaspoon ground caraway seeds

$1/8$ teaspoon red pepper flakes

I cup olive oil

$1/2$ cup fresh lemon juice (from about 4 lemons)

4 boneless, skinless chicken breast fillets, pounded evenly to $1/2$-inch thickness

2 large red onions, peeled and cut into I-inch slices

8 wooden skewers, soaked in water for 30 minutes

2 cups cooked couscous

$1/2$ cup chopped dried apricots

$1/2$ cup currants or sweetened dried cranberries

$1/2$ cup chopped green onions (white and green parts)

$1/4$ cup chopped fresh Italian parsley

1   Prepare a hot fire in your grill. Oil a perforated grill rack and set aside.

2   In a small bowl, combine the *Tunisian Grilling Spice Mixture* ingredients. Whisk to blend and set aside. In another small bowl, combine the olive oil and lemon juice. Whisk to blend and set aside.

3   Place the chicken on a doubled baking sheet and drizzle each breast with about 1 tablespoon of the olive oil and lemon juice mixture. Then lightly sprinkle both sides of each chicken breast with about 1 tablespoon of the spice mixture. Skewer each onion slice widthwise and place on the baking sheet or on a perforated grilling rack. Drizzle the onions with some of the olive oil mixture. (Reserve 2 to 3 tablespoons of the olive oil mixture for the couscous.)

4   Mix the couscous with the dried fruits, green onions, parsley, and 2 or 3 tablespoons of the reserved olive oil and lemon juice mixture.

5   Grill the chicken for about $2\frac{1}{2}$ minutes per side, turning once. Grill the onions for 3 to 4 minutes per side, turning once, or until you have good grill marks. Transfer the cooked food to the clean baking sheet. Serve with the couscous.

Asiago Grilled Chicken Breasts with Linguine Marinara

For a time-saving step, grill extra chicken one day, then prepare this recipe a couple of days later with the leftovers. Just sprinkle on the Asiago cheese at that time and give it a quick reheat in the oven while you cook the linguine. The marinara is simple to put together. The sautéed garlic and fresh basil add lots of zip to this dish. It is low-cal and extremely satisfying served in the fall or winter.

SERVES 4

4 boneless, skinless chicken breast fillets, pounded to $1/2$-inch thickness

1 tablespoon olive oil

4 tablespoons freshly grated Asiago or Romano cheese

2 tablespoons toasted bread crumbs

Kosher or sea salt and freshly ground black pepper to taste

Linguine Marinara

$1/3$ cup olive oil

4 whole cloves garlic

4 cups chopped canned Roma tomatoes

4 tablespoons chopped fresh basil

4 cloves garlic, minced

Kosher or sea salt and black pepper to taste

1 pound linguine, cooked according to package directions

4 tablespoons freshly grated Asiago cheese

You've Got Dinner!

GREEN SALAD OR STEAMED BROCCOLINI

1 Prepare a hot fire in your grill.

2 Rinse the chicken well and pat dry. Coat the chicken with the olive oil, cheese, bread crumbs, salt, and pepper. Grill over a hot fire for about $2^1/2$ minutes per side. Remove from the grill and keep warm.

3 To make the *Linguine Marinara*, add the olive oil to a large skillet over medium-high heat. Add the whole garlic cloves and brown slightly, then add the tomatoes. Simmer, stirring occasionally. Add the basil, minced garlic, salt, and pepper. Cook for 10 to 15 minutes, stirring occasionally. Add the cooked linguine to the skillet, tossing to combine, and reheat. Add the Asiago cheese and mix well. Serve at once on a large platter, topped with the golden grilled chicken.

TIME-SAVING TIARA TOUCH

Our marinara is very quick to make, but if you're feeling especially frazzled, buy a good-quality jarred tomato-basil pasta sauce to use instead.

Chicken, Prosciutto, and Bay Skewers with Minted Carrot Salad

Here's an entrée full of flavor contrasts: the salty prosciutto, the sweet and hot baste, the mellow chicken, and the fresh mint and sweet carrot with just a hint of heat. Fresh bay leaves are often available in the produce section of the grocery store. If not, you can find them at nurseries that stock bay plants. If you can't find fresh bay leaves, then use fresh sage leaves or omit them. This looks beautiful on your plate. If you like, serve the skewers atop fusilli. The Minted Carrot Salad makes a great side for just about any grilled entrée.

SERVES 4

Minted Carrot Salad

4 cups shredded carrots (about I pound)

2 tablespoons red wine vinegar

I tablespoon olive oil

$^1/_4$ teaspoon cayenne pepper

Fine kosher or sea salt and freshly ground black pepper to taste

I bunch fresh chives, snipped (about $^1/_2$ cup)

2 tablespoons chopped fresh mint leaves

Honey Mustard Baste

MAKES ABOUT I CUP

$^1/_2$ cup Dijon mustard

$^1/_4$ cup dry white wine, such as Pinot Grigio or Chardonnay

$^1/_4$ cup clover or other amber honey

4 boneless, skinless chicken breasts, cut into 2-inch pieces (about 24 pieces total)

8 slices prosciutto, cut lengthwise into thirds

8 wooden skewers, soaked in water for at least 30 minutes prior to grilling

16 fresh bay leaves

You've Got Dinner!
GRILLED CORN ON THE COB

1   Combine the *Minted Carrot Salad* ingredients in a large bowl, toss to blend, and set aside.

2   Make the *Honey Mustard Baste* by mixing together the mustard, wine, and honey in a small bowl. Set aside.

3   Prepare a hot fire in your grill.

4   Wrap each piece of chicken with a thin piece of prosciutto and arrange 3 pieces on each skewer, with a fresh bay leaf in between. Do not crowd the chicken on the skewers. Place the skewers on a doubled baking sheet.

5   Place the skewers on the grill grate and use a spoon to drizzle each skewer with the basting mixture. Cover and grill for 5 to 6 minutes. When the chicken has turned opaque on the bottom, turn the skewers and baste with a brush. Cover and cook for another 5 to 6 minutes, or until the chicken is opaque and firm all the way through. Transfer to the clean baking sheet.

6   Serve the skewers hot, discarding the bay leaves, with the carrot salad on the side.

TIME-SAVING TIARA TOUCH

To make this really easy on yourself, either buy the shredded carrots at a salad bar or shred them in your food processor.

Grilled Chicken Wings and Spuds, Southwest Style

Chicken wings are often thought of only as appetizer fare. However, they make for a scrumptious casual meal and are easy on the budget. The kids love them, too. Grilled Mango and Pineapple Salsa (page 126) or Black Bean Salsa (page 166) would be good accompaniments. Pick up some blue cheese or ranch dressing to use as a dipping sauce for the wings. A smoky Southwest flavor is easily achieved by adding a handful of water-soaked mesquite chips to your hot charcoal fire, or placing dry mesquite wood chips or pellets in a foil packet poked with holes on the grill grate over one of the burners of your gas grill.

SERVES 4

2 pounds chicken wings

1¹/₂ cups Italian dressing of your choice

¹/₂ cup chopped fresh Italian parsley or cilantro

Zest and juice of 1 lemon

¹/₂ teaspoon red pepper flakes

4 medium-size baking potatoes

1 cup mesquite wood chips or ¹/₃ cup mesquite wood pellets (see above)

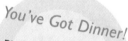

You've Got Dinner!

PLATTER OF CRUDITÉS, SUCH AS CHERRY TOMATOES, CARROT STICKS, AND GREEN BELL PEPPER STRIPS

1   Place the wings in a large zipper-top plastic bag.

2   In a 2-cup measuring cup, combine the Italian dressing, parsley, lemon zest and juice, and red pepper flakes. Pour 1 cup of the marinade into the bag of chicken. Reserve the rest of the marinade for the potatoes. Seal the bag, toss to coat, and marinate the chicken for about 20 minutes.

3   Slice each potato into 8 wedges. Place the potato wedges in a large zipper-top plastic bag and pour the rest of the marinade into the plastic bag. Seal the bag, toss to coat, and marinate for about 15 minutes.

4   Prepare a hot fire in your grill. For a gas grill, immediately place the packet of dry chips or pellets on the grill grate toward the back of the grill and close the lid. The chips and pellets will begin to smoke after 20 minutes. For a charcoal fire, sprinkle moistened wood chips or place a foil packet containing dry wood pellets on the hot coals right before grilling.

5   Grill the chicken wings on one side of the grill and the potato wedges on the other side. Turn the wings and the potatoes several times while cooking. Grill for about 20 minutes total.

6   Serve the wings and potatoes on separate platters with dipping sauces and dig in!

TIME-SAVING TIARA TOUCH

Instead of whole chicken wings, buy drummies, or cut the wing tips off, discard, and cut the wings at the joint. Grilling time will be a bit faster, about 15 minutes, and the drummies are easier to eat.

Greek-Style Chicken with Stir-Grilled Carrots, Olives, and Lemons

Stir-grilling opens up so many more possibilities for vegetables on the grill. You can use vegetables such as broccoli and carrots that you wouldn't ordinarily think to put over the coals. A zesty rub on the paillards (chicken breasts pounded to an even thickness) captures the flavors of the Greek Isles. The stir-grilled carrots, olives, and lemons make a good side for grilled fish, too.

SERVES 4

Greek Rub
MAKES 1 TABLESPOON

1 teaspoon dried oregano

1 teaspoon garlic salt

1 teaspoon freshly ground black pepper

4 boneless, skinless chicken breasts, pounded to a $^1/_2$-inch thickness

Olive oil for brushing

One 16-ounce bag baby carrots

1 lemon, thinly sliced

1 cup brine-cured olives, such as Kalamata or Niçoise

3 cloves garlic, minced

2 tablespoons fresh lemon juice

$^1/_4$ cup olive oil

You've Got Dinner!
GRILLED PITA BREAD
GREEK SALAD

1   Combine the *Greek Rub* ingredients. Brush the chicken breasts with the olive oil, then sprinkle the rub on both sides. Place the chicken on a doubled baking sheet. Set aside.

2   Prepare a hot fire in your grill.

3   Place the carrots, lemon slices, olives, garlic, lemon juice, and olive oil in a zipper-top plastic bag. Seal the bag and toss to coat. Oil both sides of a perforated grill wok and place in your sink. Pour the contents of the bag into the grill wok and let drain. Place the grill wok on the baking sheet with the chicken, and take everything out to the grill.

4   Grill the carrot mixture with the grill lid closed, tossing occasionally with wooden paddles or grill spatulas, for 20 to 25 minutes, or until the carrots have slightly browned and are crisp-tender. During the last minutes of stir-grilling, grill the chicken, turning once, for 5 minutes total. Place the cooked chicken and grill wok on the clean baking sheet to bring inside.

5   To serve, place a chicken breast and some stir-grilled vegetables on each of 4 dinner plates.

Spicy Hoisin Barbecued Chicken and Broccoli with Lemon Rice

My goodness! This is so much better than Chinese takeout. But you'll have to make it to believe it. The Hoisin Barbecue Marinade is addictive. You may want to double it to serve as a dipping sauce on the side or to drizzle over the rice. It's also delicious with grilled pork or shrimp. Remember the rule for perfect grilled boneless chicken is to pound it lightly with the rim of a saucer to an even thickness.

SERVES 4

Hoisin Barbecue Marinade
MAKES ABOUT 1 1/2 CUPS

1/2 cup hoisin sauce

1/4 cup barbecue sauce

2 tablespoons low-sodium soy sauce

2 tablespoons rice vinegar

2 teaspoons toasted sesame oil

2 teaspoons grated fresh ginger

4 cloves garlic, minced

1/2 teaspoon red pepper flakes, or more to taste

4 cups broccoli florets

4 boneless, skinless chicken breasts, pounded to 1/2-inch thickness

4 cups cooked rice

Zest and juice of 1 lemon

1 teaspoon toasted sesame seeds

1   In a small bowl, combine all of the *Hoisin Barbecue Marinade* ingredients and whisk to blend. Place the broccoli florets in a zipper-top plastic bag and add 1/2 cup of the marinade. Seal the bag, toss to coat, and set aside to

marinate. Place the chicken breasts in another zipper-top plastic bag and pour in the remaining marinade. Seal the bag, toss to coat, and marinate at room temperature for about 15 minutes.

2   Place the cooked rice in a large bowl and add the lemon zest and juice. Blend lightly with a fork. Cover with plastic wrap and set aside.

3   Prepare a hot fire in your grill. Spray a grill wok with cooking spray.

4   Place the wok in the kitchen sink. Pour the broccoli and sauce into the grill wok and let drain. (You can reuse the marinade from the broccoli, if desired.) Place the grill wok on a doubled baking sheet. Remove the chicken from the marinade and place on the baking sheet beside the wok. Discard the chicken marinade. Take the doubled sheet out to the grill.

5   Place the wok on the grill and close the lid for about 2 minutes. Open the grill and toss the broccoli with wooden paddles or grill spatulas several times while grilling, for a total of 12 to 15 minutes. Place the chicken directly on the grill grate and cook for $2^1/_2$ to 3 minutes per side. When everything is done, place the food on the clean baking sheet and carry back to the kitchen.

6   Place the broccoli in a bowl, add the toasted sesame seeds, and toss. Arrange the chicken on a platter. Reheat the rice in the microwave if needed.

Tropicana Chicken, Mango, and Pineapple Skewers with Orange-Coconut Marinade

During the colder months when tropical fruits come into season, you can get a welcome taste of the tropics in dishes like this one. We also love this marinade on shrimp and scallop skewers and on salmon and other grilled fish.

SERVES 4

Orange-Coconut Marinade
MAKES ABOUT 2 CUPS

One 14-ounce can regular or light coconut milk

1 tablespoon Thai red curry paste, or to taste

2 teaspoons freshly grated orange zest

$1/2$ cup orange juice

You've Got Dinner!
SERVE ON A BED OF STEAMED JASMINE RICE

4 boneless, skinless chicken breasts, cut into 2-inch chunks

1 medium-size ripe mango, peeled, pitted, and cut into 2-inch chunks

1 medium-size ripe pineapple, peeled, cored, and cut into 2-inch chunks

12 skewers (if using wooden skewers, soak for 30 minutes before grilling)

1   In a medium-size bowl, whisk together the *Orange-Coconut Marinade* ingredients. Place the chicken chunks in a large bowl and toss with $3/4$ cup of the marinade. Place the fruits in another large bowl and toss with $3/4$ cup of the remaining marinade. Reserve the remaining $1/2$ cup of marinade. Let the chicken and the fruits marinate for 15 minutes.

2   Oil the grill grates. Prepare a medium-hot fire in your grill.

3   Thread the chicken pieces onto 4 of the skewers. Thread the fruit pieces onto the remaining 8 skewers. Place everything on a doubled baking sheet and take out to the grill.

4 Grill the chicken skewers for 3 to 4 minutes per side, turning once, until the chicken is opaque and firm to the touch. Grill the fruit skewers for 2 minutes per side, turning once, until you have good grill marks. Place the cooked skewers on the clean baking sheet and bring inside.

5 Drizzle the skewers with the reserved marinade and serve immediately.

TIME-SAVING TIARA TOUCH

Grill 2 or 3 extra skewers of chicken and you've got the makings of Tropical Chicken and Rice Salad (page 58) to serve as a meal later in the week.

Grilled Chicken Pasta with Tomatoes, Fresh Thyme, and Brine-Cured Olives

When you have leftover grilled chicken, make this simple dish that bursts with the flavor of brine-cured olives. A chilled rosé from France, Spain, or Portugal would be delightful with this dish.

SERVES 4 TO 6

3 tablespoons olive oil

1 pound leftover grilled boneless, skinless chicken breast, thinly sliced

5 medium-size ripe tomatoes, peeled, seeded, and chopped (about 2 cups)

1 1/2 cups brine-cured Kalamata olives, drained, pitted, and chopped

2 teaspoons fresh thyme leaves

1/2 teaspoon kosher or sea salt

1/2 teaspoon freshly ground black pepper

1/4 teaspoon red pepper flakes

8 ounces small shell or tubular pasta, cooked according to package directions

3/4 cup reserved pasta water

1 cup freshly grated Parmesan or Asiago cheese

1 tablespoon chopped fresh Italian parsley, for garnish

You've Got Dinner!

ROMAINE LETTUCE AND RADICCHIO SALAD WITH A BALSAMIC VINAIGRETTE

1   Pour the olive oil into a large pot over medium-high heat. Stir in the grilled chicken, tomatoes, olives, thyme, salt, black pepper, and red pepper flakes. Blend well and heat through. Add the pasta and pasta water and heat through.

2   Spoon the mixture into a casserole or large shallow serving bowl. Sprinkle the top with the cheese and sprinkle with the chopped parsley. Serve warm or at room temperature.

TIME-SAVING TIARA TOUCH

This can easily be made earlier in the day and placed in an ovenproof casserole, covered with foil, and refrigerated. Just warm it in the oven prior to serving.

Abruzzi-Style Grilled Chicken with Zucchini and Yellow Summer Squash

You get big flavor and lots of color in this one-dish meal. The chunky, hearty tomato sauce is redolent of garlic, rosemary, and olives in the manner of the Abruzzi region of Italy. We're big on boneless chicken thighs for this dish, because their meatiness can stand up to the bold flavor of the sauce. But if chicken breasts are on sale, go for them. And if you grill $2^{1}/_{2}$ pounds of chicken instead of $1^{1}/_{2}$, you'll have leftovers to use for Grilled Chicken Pasta with Tomatoes, Fresh Thyme, and Brine-Cured Olives (page 160) or to shred and use in salads and sandwiches.

SERVES 4

Abruzzi Sauce
MAKES ABOUT 4 $^{1}/_{2}$ CUPS

- 1 tablespoon olive oil
- 2 large cloves garlic, minced
- $^{1}/_{4}$ teaspoon red pepper flakes
- 1 teaspoon dried rosemary
- $^{1}/_{4}$ cup dry red or white wine
- One 28-ounce can tomatoes (we like fire-roasted from Muir Glen)
- 1 cup pitted oil-cured black olives

- 1 medium-size zucchini, ends trimmed
- 1 medium-size yellow summer squash, ends trimmed
- $1^{1}/_{2}$ pounds boneless, skinless chicken thighs or breasts
- Olive oil for brushing
- 1 tablespoon fresh lemon juice
- Kosher or sea salt and freshly ground black pepper to taste

You've Got Dinner!

SIDE OF PASTA OR GRILLED GARLIC BREAD

1   Prepare a medium-hot fire in your grill.

2   To make the *Abruzzi Sauce*, heat the oil in a large skillet over medium-high heat. Add the garlic and red pepper flakes and sauté for 1 minute, or until you begin to smell the garlic. Stir in the remaining ingredients and bring to a boil. Reduce the heat to medium and cook, stirring, until the sauce reduces and thickens, about 20 minutes. Set aside.

3   Meanwhile, slice the zucchini and yellow summer squash lengthwise into $^1/_2$-inch-thick strips and place on a small baking sheet. On a separate doubled baking sheet, brush the chicken with olive oil, drizzle with lemon juice, then season with salt and pepper. Bring both trays out to the grill.

4   Grill the zucchini and yellow summer squash strips for 3 to 4 minutes per side, turning once with grill tongs. Transfer to a clean baking sheet. Grill the chicken for 4 to 5 minutes per side, turning once with grill tongs. Transfer to the baking sheet with the squash and bring everything back inside.

5   To serve, divide the sauce among 4 plates and top with the chicken. Quickly chop the zucchini and squash, season with salt and pepper, and arrange around the perimeter of the sauce. Serve hot.

Grilled Turkey, Cranberry, and Brie Quesadillas

Colorful, rich, and yummy, these quesadillas take the idea of fast food into another culinary dimension. Keep cranberries on hand all year long by freezing bags of them to thaw and use when you like, as we do.

SERVES 4

Cranberry-Orange Salsa
MAKES ABOUT 3 CUPS

2 cups fresh or frozen and thawed cranberries

2 large oranges, peeled, seeded, and chopped

2 tablespoons honey

I pound turkey breast cutlets, cut into strips

2 tablespoons olive oil

Kosher or sea salt to taste

Lemon pepper to taste

2 cups (about 10 ounces) chopped Brie cheese (rind removed)

Eight 8-inch flour tortillas

You've Got Dinner!

MICRO-BAKED SWEET POTATOES

GREEN SALAD

1   Combine all the *Cranberry-Orange Salsa* ingredients in a food processor or blender and pulse until coarsely chopped. Cover and chill until ready to serve.

2   Prepare a medium-hot fire in your grill. Oil a perforated grill rack and have it ready by the grill.

3   Place the turkey strips with the olive oil and salt and lemon pepper in a zipper-top plastic bag, seal, and toss to coat. Place the bag on a baking sheet, along with the Brie, salsa, and flour tortillas, and take everything to the grill.

4   Place the turkey strips on the prepared grill rack and grill for 5 to 8 minutes, turning with a grill spatula, until the turkey is no longer pink in the center and reaches an internal temperature of 170°F on an instant-read thermometer.

5   Meanwhile, spread $1/2$ cup of Brie over each of 4 tortillas. When the turkey is done, sprinkle $1/2$ cup of turkey and $1/2$ cup of salsa over the Brie. Place a second tortilla over the top of the turkey-cranberry mixture and gently press down. Place 2 quesadillas on the grill rack, close the lid, and grill for 5 to 7 minutes, or until the cheese has melted and the bottom tortilla has grill marks. Transfer to the baking sheet and cover with foil to keep warm. Grill the remaining 2 quesadillas.

6   To serve, cut each quesadilla into 6 wedges and serve hot.

TIME-SAVING TIARA TOUCH

The Cranberry-Orange Salsa can be made in advance. It will keep in the refrigerator in an airtight container for up to 2 weeks.

Sassy Cilantro Salsa Turkey Steaks with Black Bean Salsa, Too!

Karen plays bridge and has tried to teach Judith, but her English major/non-math genes just don't get it. However, Judith is all in favor of the "bridge" recipes that come our way. These two salsas are from Karen's bridge buddy Pam Molnar. They are easy, tasty, and pretty healthy, too. So let the salsas do triple duty as a topping on grilled meat, as a dip with tortilla chips, and as a side dish.

SERVES 4

Four 4- to 6-ounce turkey breast tenderloin steaks, $^1/_2$ inch thick

Olive oil for brushing

$^1/_2$ teaspoon garlic salt

Freshly ground black pepper to taste

3 teaspoons fresh lime juice

$^1/_4$ cup chopped cilantro

3 cups cooked rice

Sassy Cilantro Salsa
MAKES ABOUT 4 CUPS

1 large tomato, chopped

5 green onions, chopped (white and green parts)

One 4-ounce can chopped black olives

One 4-ounce can chopped green chiles, drained

$^1/_2$ cup chopped fresh cilantro

$^1/_3$ cup Italian salad dressing of your choice

2 cups finely shredded Monterey Jack cheese

Black Bean Salsa
MAKES ABOUT 4 CUPS

One 15-ounce can black beans, rinsed and drained

One 15.25-ounce can whole kernel corn, drained

³/₄ cup diced red bell pepper

5 green onions, finely chopped (white and green parts)

¹/₄ cup chopped fresh cilantro

Zest and juice of 1 lime

Zest and juice of 1 lemon

2 teaspoons ground cumin

¹/₄ teaspoon garlic salt

4 lettuce leaves, such as Boston

1 Rinse and pat dry the turkey tenderloin steaks. Place on a doubled baking sheet and lightly coat with the olive oil. Sprinkle evenly with the garlic salt and season with pepper.

2 Add the lime juice and chopped cilantro to the cooked rice, fluffing gently with a fork to combine. Keep warm on the stovetop.

3 Prepare a medium-hot fire in your grill.

4 To make the *Sassy Cilantro Salsa*, in a medium-size bowl, combine the tomato, onions, black olives, green chiles, cilantro, and Italian dressing. Stir to blend and set aside. (Stir in the cheese right before it is to be used.)

5 To make the *Black Bean Salsa*, in a large bowl, combine the beans, corn, red bell pepper, green onions, and cilantro. In a small bowl, combine the lime and lemon zest and juice, cumin, and garlic salt. Pour over the bean mixture and toss gently to coat. Serve at room temperature or chill in the refrigerator for up to 3 days.

6 Grill the turkey steaks for 4 to 5 minutes per side, or until the turkey is no longer pink. Turkey is done when an instant-read thermometer inserted into the meatiest part registers 160° to 165°F. Transfer the turkey to the clean baking sheet.

7 On each of 4 dinner plates, place a turkey steak and one-fourth of the rice. Stir the cheese into the cilantro salsa and spoon it over the turkey to your liking. Serve a portion of the black bean salsa next to it on a lettuce leaf.

Grilled Turkey Steaks with Quick Peperonata and Parmesan Couscous

The peperonata here goes beautifully with both the turkey and the couscous and brings a rich red color to the whiteness of the rest of the food. Our recipe uses cans or jars of fire-roasted red bell peppers and tomatoes. If "fire-roasted" isn't available, buy products labeled "Italian-style." We like the fire-roasted because there is actual charred skin on them, which is very tasty. The peperonata takes all of 10 minutes to cook and the couscous about 5 minutes. Serve a salad on the side, if you like, but there must be bread with this meal to dredge in the flavorful sauce.

SERVES 4

Four 4- to 6-ounce turkey breast tenderloin steaks, $1/2$ inch thick

Olive oil for brushing

Kosher or sea salt and freshly ground black pepper to taste

Quick Peperonata

MAKES ABOUT 4 CUPS

2 tablespoons olive oil

2 cloves garlic, chopped

1 large red onion, chopped

One 12-ounce jar fire-roasted red bell peppers, chopped

One 14.5-ounce can fire-roasted chopped tomatoes

1 tablespoon capers

$1/4$ teaspoon red pepper flakes

Kosher or sea salt and freshly ground black pepper to taste

One 5.6-ounce box Parmesan-flavored couscous, cooked according to package directions

1 Rinse and pat dry the turkey tenderloin steaks. Place on a doubled baking sheet, lightly coat with the olive oil, and season with salt and pepper.

2 Prepare a medium-hot fire in your grill.

3 To make the *Quick Peperonata*, in a large sauté pan, heat the olive oil over medium heat and add the garlic and onion. Sauté for about 5 minutes. Add the red bell peppers, tomatoes, capers, and red pepper flakes. Heat, and season with salt and pepper.

4 Grill the turkey steaks for about 5 minutes per side, until the turkey is no longer pink. Turkey is done when an instant-read thermometer inserted into the meatiest part registers 160° to 165°F. Transfer to the clean baking sheet.

5 On each of 4 dinner plates, place a turkey steak and one-fourth of the couscous. Spoon the peperonata over both, to your liking, and serve immediately.

TIME-SAVING TIARA TOUCH

Make extra peperonata and use it to top toasted bread as a quick hors d'oeuvre for weekend company, or to top lunchtime turkey or roast beef sandwiches.

Grilled Turkey Tenderloins and Skewered Brussels Sprouts with Basil Butter

Turkey breast tenderloins weigh in at about $^3/_4$ pound per half breast. The meat is very lean, thus basting with olive oil or butter during grilling keeps the outer meat moist and tender. The simplicity of the Basil Butter is drop-dead great. You'll make this over and over again, especially if you grow your own basil. Be sure to serve crusty bread whenever you offer these yummy butter sauces. Okay! Okay! So some of you don't like Brussels sprouts. Then switch to some other vegetable. However, we are both amazed at how many people think they don't like Brussels sprouts and change their minds when they try fresh small sprouts that have been cooked to perfection.

SERVES 4

Two 1$^1/_2$-pound turkey breast tenderloins

2 to 3 tablespoons olive oil

Kosher or sea salt and freshly ground black pepper to taste

1$^1/_2$ pounds Brussels sprouts, ends trimmed

4 metal skewers

Basil Butter
MAKES ABOUT I CUP

$^3/_4$ cup (1$^1/_2$ sticks) unsalted butter

1$^1/_2$ cups fresh basil leaves

You've Got Dinner!
WILD RICE OR CRUSTY FRENCH BREAD

1 Rinse and pat dry the turkey breasts. Place on a doubled baking sheet. Lightly brush both sides of the turkey with olive oil and season with salt and pepper. Set aside.

2 Place the Brussels sprouts in a large saucepan, and just cover with cold water. Bring to a boil over high heat and cook for about 5 minutes. Drain in

a colander. When cool, thread one-fourth of the sprouts onto each of 4 skewers, lightly brush with olive oil, and season with salt and pepper.

3 Prepare a medium-hot fire in your grill.

4 To prepare the *Basil Butter*, melt the butter in a small saucepan over low heat. Right before serving, reheat the butter until it is bubbling, add the basil leaves, and cook for about 2 minutes. The basil should remain bright green.

5 Grill the turkey tenderloins for about 10 minutes per side, until the turkey is no longer pink. Turkey is done when an instant-read thermometer inserted into the meatiest part registers 160° to 165°F. Grill the skewered Brussels sprouts at the same time for 8 to 10 minutes, until lightly browned. Place the turkey and sprouts on the clean baking sheet and bring inside.

6 Let the turkey rest for 3 to 4 minutes, then slice into 1-inch-thick slices. Place an equal amount of slices on each of 4 plates along with a skewer of sprouts. Drizzle the basil butter over all and serve immediately.

Asian Turkey Tenderloins with Bok Choy Salad

It's nice to revisit old recipes like this one using ramen noodles. The dressing is very good, and we've increased the amount so there is enough to marinate the turkey tenderloins as well. When slicing a tenderloin, we advise cutting thick slices, to keep the meat warmer and juicier. We love getting the kids in our families involved with meal preparation. So don't forget to have them help you crunch the noodles. Pretty soon they'll be making the whole salad. Now that's both a real time-saver and a gift to give this generation of fast-food junkies.

SERVES 4

Two 1½-pound turkey breast tenderloins

1 cup sugar

¾ cup rice vinegar

1½ cups olive oil

3 tablespoons low-sodium soy sauce

2 teaspoons sesame oil

Two 3-ounce packages ramen noodles

½ cup (1 stick) unsalted butter

½ cup sliced almonds

3 tablespoons sesame seeds

1 head bok choy, chopped

15 green onions, chopped (white and green parts)

You've Got Dinner!

STEAMED RICE OR CHINESE NOODLES

1   Rinse the turkey and place in a large zipper-top plastic bag.

2   Combine the sugar, vinegar, olive oil, soy sauce, and sesame oil in a large bowl and mix well. Pour ¾ cup of the mixture over the turkey, seal the bag, toss to coat, and marinate in the refrigerator for 20 to 30 minutes. Chill the remaining dressing, covered, until needed.

3   Prepare a medium-hot fire in your grill.

4   Break up the ramen noodles in the unopened packages. Discard the seasoning packets or reserve for another use. In a large skillet, melt the butter and sauté the noodles, almonds, and sesame seeds for 4 to 5 minutes. Set aside.

5   Combine the bok choy and green onions in a large bowl. Add the reserved dressing and mix well.

6   Remove the turkey from the marinade and discard the marinade. Place on a doubled baking sheet and carry out to the grill. Grill the tenderloins for 17 to 18 minutes total, turning halfway through the cooking time. The internal temperature should register 160° to 165°F on an instant-read thermometer. Transfer to the clean baking sheet.

7   When ready to serve, stir the ramen noodle mixture into the salad mixture and spoon onto one side of each of 4 plates. Slice the turkey into 1-inch-thick slices and fan them on the opposite side of the plate.

TIME-SAVING TIARA TOUCH

Instead of bok choy, you can substitute a 6-ounce package of precut cabbage or a bunch of celery, thinly sliced in your food processor.

Grilled Turkey Tenderloins with Grilled Fennel and New Potatoes with Spicy Lemon Butter

This is a lean and mean supper. The turkey and fennel are low-cal and low-carb. So much so, that the potatoes and drizzle of butter hardly count!

SERVES 4

Spicy Lemon Butter
MAKES ABOUT ¹/₂ CUP

¹/₂ cup (I stick) unsalted butter, melted

Zest and juice of I lemon

I teaspoon Cajun or other zesty seasoning mix

I pound new potatoes

Four 4- to 6-ounce turkey breast tenderloin steaks, cut ¹/₂ inch thick

2 fennel bulbs, ends and feathery tops trimmed, sliced in half

Olive oil for brushing

Fine kosher or sea salt and freshly ground black pepper to taste

1 Prepare a medium to medium-hot fire in your grill.

2 Combine the *Spicy Lemon Butter* ingredients and set aside.

3 Micro-cook the potatoes on high for 6 minutes, or until the potatoes can be easily pierced with a knife. Set aside to cool slightly.

4 Rub the turkey tenderloins, the fennel, and the par-cooked potatoes with olive oil and season with salt and pepper. Place the turkey on a plate and place everything on a doubled baking sheet to take out to the grill.

5 Grill the turkey, turning once after the first 6 or 7 minutes, for about 12 to 15 minutes total, or until no longer pink. Turkey is done when an instant-read thermometer inserted into the meatiest part registers 160°F. At the same time, grill the fennel and potatoes, turning several times, until browned all over and tender. Remove the food to the clean baking sheet. Serve the turkey alongside the fennel and new potatoes. Drizzle all with the spicy lemon butter.

TIME-SAVING TIARA TOUCH

Small, fresh, and tender vegetables cook more quickly on the grill and taste better, too.

Spicy Grilled Turkey Sausage with Cannellini Beans, Tomatoes, and Angel Hair Pasta

Our choice of sausage for this dish is Italian-style hot turkey sausages, though of course you may use mild versions. You get loads of flavor with less fat. This is a great-looking dish to serve family-style on a large, pretty serving platter. A nice touch to finish it off is to sprinkle it all with gremolata, which you can easily make by combining 1 cup of chopped fresh Italian parsley, the zest of 1 lemon, and 1 minced garlic clove. Salad and bread are optional side dishes. Enjoy!

SERVES 4

4 Italian-style hot turkey sausages

4 tablespoons olive oil

2 or 3 cloves garlic, minced

One 14.5-ounce can fire-roasted chopped tomatoes

One 15-ounce can cannellini beans, drained and rinsed

$^1/_4$ cup freshly chopped Italian parsley

$^1/_4$ cup freshly chopped basil

Kosher or sea salt and freshly ground black pepper to taste

1 pound angel hair pasta, cooked according to package directions

1   Place the sausages on a doubled baking sheet and lightly coat with 1 table-spoon of the olive oil so they do not stick to the grill.

2   Prepare a hot fire in your grill.

3   In a large sauté pan, heat the remaining 3 tablespoons of olive oil over medium heat. Add the garlic and sauté for 3 or 4 minutes. Add the tomatoes, beans, parsley, and basil. Let the sauce simmer while you are out at the grill. Season with salt and pepper.

4   Grill the sausages for 12 to 15 minutes, turning several times on the grill, until nicely browned and cooked through. The internal temperature should register 170°F on an instant-read thermometer. Place the cooked sausages on the clean baking sheet and bring inside.

5   Place the drained pasta on the serving platter. Top with the warm tomato and bean sauce, and set the sausages on top. Serve immediately.

TIME-SAVING TIARA TOUCH

Keep several different kinds of canned beans in your pantry to have on hand for recipes like this and for salsas and side dishes.

Stir-Grilled Turkey Picadillo Wraps with Jicama, Carrot, and Orange Salad

"Picadillo" is a Cuban term meaning a chili-like dish of meats cut into small bites. A picadillo mixture usually contains both savory and sweet ingredients, such as olives and raisins, and is sometimes used for empanada fillings. In this easy weekday dish, you stir-grill the ground turkey, then combine it with the no-cook sauce for a big-flavor dish.

SERVES 4

Picadillo Sauce
MAKES ABOUT 2 CUPS

 I medium-size onion, chopped

 I medium-size red bell pepper, seeded and chopped

 One 10-ounce can tomatoes with green chiles, undrained

 $^3/_4$ cup chopped pimiento-stuffed green olives

 $^1/_2$ cup golden raisins

 I tablespoon capers

 I tablespoon Worcestershire sauce

Jicama, Carrot, and Orange Salad

 I medium-size jicama, peeled and shredded or julienned

 2 large carrots, shredded or julienned

 I medium-size orange, peeled and roughly sectioned

 I tablespoon fresh lime juice

 2 tablespoons olive oil

 Fine kosher or sea salt and freshly ground black pepper to taste

1 pound ground turkey

1 teaspoon ground cumin

1 tablespoon vegetable oil

Fine kosher or sea salt and freshly ground black pepper to taste

8 small flour tortillas

1   In a large bowl, stir together the *Picadillo Sauce* ingredients and set aside.

2   In a second large bowl, stir together the *Jicama, Carrot, and Orange Salad* ingredients and set aside.

3   In a third large bowl, mix together the turkey, cumin, vegetable oil, and salt and pepper with a wooden spoon or your hands. Oil a grill wok on both sides and spoon the turkey mixture into the wok. Place the wok on a doubled baking sheet.

4   Prepare a hot fire in your grill.

5   Stir-grill the turkey, using wooden paddles or grill spatulas, for 15 to 20 minutes, or until the turkey is cooked through. Place the wok on the clean baking sheet and bring inside.

6   Add the turkey to the bowl with the picadillo sauce and mix well. Place a spoonful of the turkey mixture in the center of each tortilla and roll up. Serve with the salad on the side.

TIME-SAVING TIARA TOUCH

If you have a food processor, by all means use it to shred the jicama and carrots for the tart and tangy salad.

Hooked on Fish

When we wrote our cookbook *Fish & Shellfish, Grilled & Smoked* (The Harvard Common Press, 2002), we grilled and smoked everything from amberjack to zebra fish. So we know how essentially easy most fish are to grill. If you still doubt us, consider this: you can have a fabulous grilled fish dinner in less than 10 minutes of grilling time. Don't you want to believe now?

One secret to grilling most fish is to measure the thickness of the fillet or steak first, because that determines your grilling time. The rule of thumb is 10 minutes of total grilling time per inch of thickness. There are only a few exceptions to that rule. Meaty fish such as tuna and swordfish, for example, take even less time. We'll tell you in every recipe, however, just how long to grill your fish.

The second secret is to brush the grill grates with vegetable oil (or use the wonderful pre-moistened, disposable Grate Chef Grill Wipes, available at barbecue and grill stores and in catalogs). Also, brush the fish with olive oil. If a fish is delicate (walleye pike or turbot, for example), use an oiled perforated grill rack as extra insurance.

The third secret is to grill fillets flesh side down first. You can tell which is the skin side and which is the flesh side by just looking at the fillet. Grilling flesh side down first means that the more delicate side is done first, leaving the slightly more sturdy skin side for last. Fillets are easier to take off the grill when you use this technique.

The BBQ Queens are not worriers by nature, but we realize not everyone is like us. (We only worry about our tiaras getting dented or lost during travel.) If you want to worry about something, worry about getting your fish *too done*. Don't worry about undercooking it. Remember that it will keep cooking after you remove it from the grill, and even if you do manage to undercook fish on the grill, you can always zap it in the microwave for 30 seconds or so. If you overcook it, there's no remedy.

Lemon Lover's Rosemary Haddock with Tomato Gratin

Save this recipe for late summer or early fall, when the tomato harvest is coming to an end and you're ready for something other than fresh sliced. Here, the BBQ Queens offer our version of tomatoes au gratin on the grill. It's really worth it to make the time to pulse a couple of pieces of artisan bread in the food processor with the parsley, garlic, and cheese. Then simply sprinkle the crumb mixture on top of each slice of grilled tomato. Rosemary is at its glory at the end of summer, too. The Lemon Lover's Rosemary Rub is not a dry rub, so it will not keep indefinitely. Instead, make up enough to use within 2 weeks.

SERVES 4

Four 6- to 8-ounce haddock fillets

2 to 3 tablespoons olive oil

8 tomato slices, $^3/_4$ inch thick, just ripe and still very firm

2 or 3 slices fresh artisan bread (we like rosemary olive)

$^1/_4$ cup chopped parsley

2 cloves garlic, minced

$^1/_4$ cup grated Romano cheese

Lemon Lover's Rosemary Rub
MAKES ABOUT $^1/_2$ CUP

2 teaspoons lemon zest (from about 2 lemons)

1 tablespoon fresh rosemary leaves, minced

2 cloves garlic, minced

$^1/_2$ cup coarse kosher or sea salt

1 teaspoon freshly ground black pepper

Lemon Butter Drizzle
MAKES ABOUT $^2/_3$ CUP

$^1/_2$ cup (1 stick) unsalted butter

$^1/_4$ cup fresh lemon juice (from about 2 lemons)

You've Got Dinner!
COUSCOUS,
ROASTED POTATOES, OR
CRUSTY BREAD

1   Rinse the fish fillets and pat dry. Place on a platter, lightly coat each fillet with some of the olive oil, and set aside. Place the tomatoes on a separate platter, brush each side with the remaining olive oil, and set aside.

2   Tear the slices of bread into small pieces and pulse to crumbs in a food processor. Add the parsley and garlic and pulse again. Then add the Romano cheese, pulse, and place the crumb mixture in a small bowl.

3   Again in the food processor (no need to clean it), combine all the **Lemon Lover's Rosemary Rub** ingredients and pulse 2 or 3 times to blend. Pour the mixture into a glass jar with a tight-fitting lid and store any leftovers in the refrigerator.

4   Prepare a hot fire in your grill. Set an oiled perforated grill rack over the fire for the fish fillets.

5   To make the **Lemon Butter Drizzle**, in a small saucepan, melt the butter and add the lemon juice.

6   Sprinkle the oiled fish fillets with a little bit of the rosemary rub. Place the fish, tomatoes, and bread crumb mixture on a doubled baking sheet and take out to the grill. Place the tomato slices on one side of the grill and the fish fillets on the preheated grill rack.

7   Grill the fish fillets, flesh side down first, for about $3^1/_2$ minutes, then turn them once and finish grilling them, about another 4 minutes. They are done when opaque and just beginning to flake when touched with a fork. Grill the tomatoes for 3 to 4 minutes on one side, then turn them and liberally sprinkle the bread crumb mixture on the grilled side. Grill for another 3 to 4 minutes. Remove the fish and tomatoes to the clean baking sheet.

8   To serve, place a fish fillet on each of 4 plates. Place 2 grilled tomato slices beside the fish. Sprinkle a little bit of the rosemary rub over all and top with the lemon butter drizzle.

Halibut en Papillote

The flavors and colors of Italy come through in this surprise package. The term *en papillote* usually means a food baked in a wrapping of parchment paper, but on the grill, the BBQ Queens use heavy-duty aluminum foil. Open the foil package and it's instant therapy—aroma-, visual, and gustatory therapy all at once. How great is that? We recommend serving the rest of the wine (we suggest Pinot Grigio or Chardonnay) to toast an impressively simple meal. For a different version of this dish, put leftover Sofrito (page 94) or Quick Peperonata (page 168) on top of the fish instead of the mushrooms and tomatoes.

SERVES 4

Four 6- to 8-ounce halibut fillets (or use pompano, grouper, bluefish, red snapper, cod, or catfish)

2 cups sliced fresh white mushrooms

2 cups canned Italian plum tomatoes, drained

1/4 cup chopped fresh tarragon

1/4 cup chopped fresh Italian parsley

1/4 cup dry white wine

1/4 cup extra virgin olive oil

You've Got Dinner!
STEAMED BABY POTATOES OR ITALIAN BREAD

1   Prepare a very hot fire in your grill. You'll want the temperature to be as close to 450°F as you can get it.

2   Take four 18 x 18-inch sheets of heavy-duty aluminum foil, lay each sheet of foil on a flat surface, and place a fish fillet in the middle. Top each with 1/2 cup each of the sliced mushrooms and tomatoes, and 1 tablespoon each of tarragon, parsley, white wine, and olive oil. Wrap and seal the foil securely to form 4 packets.

3   Grill the packets, seam side up, with the grill lid down, for 14 to 16 minutes. Do not turn. To serve, place a packet on each plate, let cool slightly, then open. If you wish, you can transfer the contents to the plate and discard the foil or simply eat from the foil itself.

TIME-SAVING TIARA TOUCH

The fish packets can be prepared and refrigerated up to 1 day ahead, if you wish.

Grilled Halibut and Pineapple with Cilantro Red Pepper Relish

How often do we hear that accomplished grill mavens aren't sure how to grill fish? It's just so simple! Our rule of thumb is to cook most fish for 10 minutes per inch of thickness, turning only once halfway through the grilling time. Marinate fish for only up to 30 minutes. Make sure the grill grates are lightly oiled. And a little oil on the fish helps keep it from sticking, too. Halibut is a creamy white, mild-flavored fish. Pairing it with the vibrant flavors of grilled pineapple and the red pepper relish makes for a tasty and visual feast. Serve this with a refreshing Sauvignon Blanc.

SERVES 4

Four 6- to 8-ounce halibut fillets

2 tablespoons olive oil

Coarse kosher or sea salt to taste

8 fresh pineapple slices, $^1/_2$ inch thick

Cilantro Red Pepper Relish
MAKES ABOUT 2 CUPS

$^1/_2$ cup chopped cilantro

I large red bell pepper, chopped

I large yellow bell pepper, chopped

Zest and juice of I lime

$^1/_2$ teaspoon red pepper flakes (optional)

You've Got Dinner!
STEAMED RICE OR SEMOLINA BREAD

I   Brush the fillets with the olive oil and set on a doubled baking sheet. Sprinkle with the salt. Place the pineapple on a separate plate and set aside.

2   Prepare a hot fire in your grill.

3 In the meantime, in a medium-size bowl, combine all of the *Cilantro Red Pepper Relish* ingredients. Toss and set aside.

4 Grill the halibut, flesh side down first, about 5 minutes per side, turning once halfway through the grilling time, until opaque and just beginning to flake when tested with a fork. Place the cooked halibut on the clean baking sheet. At the same time the fillets are on the grill, grill the pineapple for 2 to 3 minutes per side and place the cooked pineapple on its original plate.

5 Serve the halibut with 2 slices of grilled pineapple to the side of each plate. Spoon the relish into the center of each pineapple slice and sprinkle a little bit over the fish, too.

TIME-SAVING TIARA TOUCH

You really need fresh pineapple for this recipe, not canned, which may fall apart on the grill. Buy peeled and cored fresh pineapple in your grocery store's produce department.

Grilled Mahi Mahi with Black Rice, Kiwis, and Star Fruit

Any firm- to moderately firm-fleshed fish can be substituted for the mahi mahi, a mild white fish that contrasts beautifully with the black rice. The pinkish colors of shrimp and salmon would also have great eye appeal and flavor with a contrasting rice. Black rice can be found at Asian markets, at some grocers, in the bulk grain aisle of Whole Food Markets, and in gourmet shops. If you can't find it, you can use wild rice, pecan rice, or red rice. They all have similar nutty flavors. Be sure to begin cooking the rice first, because it takes about 45 minutes to cook until soft. Slice a couple of kiwis and star fruit to serve on the side, and dinner is done.

SERVES 4

1 cup raw black rice

Four 6- to 8-ounce mahi mahi fillets

Orange Zest Vinaigrette
MAKES ABOUT 1 ¹/₂ CUPS

Zest and juice of 2 medium-size oranges

2 tablespoons Dijon mustard

3 tablespoons rice vinegar

¹/₄ cup amber honey, such as clover or wildflower

1 cup vegetable oil

¹/₂ teaspoon kosher or sea salt, or to taste

2 kiwi fruits

2 star fruits

1 medium-size white or yellow onion, finely chopped

1 cup dried apricots, snipped into small pieces with kitchen shears

¹/₂ cup golden raisins

1   Cook the rice according to the package directions. While the rice is cooking, place the mahi mahi fillets in a glass dish.

2   In a glass jar with a tight-fitting lid, combine the *Orange Zest Vinaigrette* ingredients. Shake to blend and pour about half of the vinaigrette over the mahi mahi fillets. Reserve the rest to drizzle over the cooked fish and rice.

3   Peel the kiwis and slice. Also slice the star fruit. Set aside.

4   Prepare a hot fire in your grill.

5   In a medium-size bowl, mix the onion, apricots, and golden raisins. When the rice is cooked, drain it well and pour the warm rice over the onion-fruit mixture. Cover and let sit at room temperature for 10 or 15 minutes while you are at the grill.

6   Grill the fish, flesh side down first, about 5 minutes per side, turning once halfway through the grilling time, until it is opaque and just beginning to flake when tested with a fork.

7   To serve, mound the black rice in the center of each of 4 plates. Angle the fillet over part of the rice. Overlap the kiwi and star fruit slices to the side. Drizzle all with the reserved vinaigrette.

TIME-SAVING TIARA TOUCH

Cook up a quantity of black or wild rice, then freeze it in 2-cup measures to have on hand. Then just thaw, reheat, and serve.

Grilled Salmon with Stir-Grilled Asian Cabbage and Shiitake Mushrooms

You'll feel very virtuous when you eat this healthy entrée, if you're not already beguiled by the beautiful, sensuous colors: coral salmon, pale jade cabbage, and earthy brown mushrooms. Being good does have its rewards. But if you must sin, add the easy and luscious Blender Hollandaise on page 75 or the Quick Aioli on page 192, sip a glass of buttery Chardonnay, and make no apologies. The stir-grilled mushrooms and cabbage are also great with grilled chicken.

SERVES 4

One 1-pound salmon fillet, about 1 inch thick

Olive oil for brushing

Fine kosher or sea salt and freshly ground white pepper to taste

1³/₄ cups coarsely chopped Chinese cabbage or bok choy

1 cup shiitake or cremini mushrooms, coarsely chopped

1 cup coarsely chopped green onions (white parts with some of the green)

1 clove garlic, minced

3 tablespoons soy sauce

2 teaspoons toasted sesame oil

2 tablespoons vegetable oil

1   Prepare a hot fire in your grill. Lightly oil a large grill wok on both sides and set aside.

2   Brush the salmon with the olive oil and season with the salt and white pepper. Place on a doubled baking sheet.

3   Place the cabbage, mushrooms, and green onions in a large zipper-top plastic bag. In a small bowl, whisk the garlic, soy sauce, and oils together. Pour the soy mixture over the vegetables, seal the bag, and shake to blend. Place a grill wok in your sink and pour the contents of the bag into the wok. Let drain for a minute or two, then place the wok on the doubled baking sheet.

4 Stir-grill the vegetables, turning occasionally with wooden paddles or grill spatulas, for 15 to 20 minutes, or until the cabbage is tender. Toward the end of the stir-grilling time, grill the salmon fillet, flesh side down first, for 4 minutes. Turn and grill the salmon another 2 to 4 minutes, or until the fish begins to flake when tested with a fork in the thickest part of the fillet. Place the grill wok and cooked salmon on the clean baking sheet.

5 To serve, portion the fillet into 4 pieces. Serve the stir-grilled vegetables alongside the salmon.

Char-Grilled Salmon and Baby Squash with Quick Aioli

Wild salmon is often a gorgeous ruby red. Get it if you can. Otherwise, farm-raised salmon will do just fine and is kinder to your pocketbook. An assortment of baby squash, such as zucchini, pattypan, and yellow crookneck, grill at the same time with the fish and are divine served with the aioli and a crisp Pinot Grigio or earthy Provençal rosé. Offer good, crusty bread at the table to help mop up the luscious aioli. Save any leftovers for a grilled salmon and vegetable salad topped with the aioli or your favorite vinaigrette. If you can't find whole baby squash, buy regular zucchini and yellow summer squash, cut them into 2-inch chunks, and thread them onto skewers to cook for the same amount of time.

SERVES 6

Quick Aioli
MAKES ABOUT 2 CUPS

2 cups mayonnaise

Juice and zest of 1 lemon

2 cloves garlic, minced

2 tablespoons chopped fresh basil

Six 6-ounce salmon fillets, skin on

4 tablespoons olive oil

$^1/_2$ teaspoon freshly ground white pepper

$^1/_2$ teaspoon seasoned black pepper, such as Lawry's

$^1/_2$ teaspoon garlic salt

1 pound assorted whole baby squash, such as zucchini, pattypan, and yellow crookneck

Kosher or sea salt and freshly ground black pepper to taste

1   To make the *Quick Aioli*, in a small bowl, combine the mayonnaise, lemon juice and zest, garlic, and basil. Stir and chill until ready to serve.

2   Prepare a hot fire in your grill. Oil a perforated grill rack and set aside.

3   Lightly coat the salmon fillets with about 2 tablespoons of the olive oil, then sprinkle the flesh side with the peppers and garlic salt. In a bowl, toss the baby squash with the remaining 2 tablespoons of olive oil and the salt and pepper. Place everything on a doubled baking sheet and take out to the grill.

4   Grill the salmon, flesh side down first, for about 5 minutes. Turn once and grill for another 5 minutes. (Or grill 10 minutes per inch of thickness, turning once, until the fish flakes easily.) At the same time, place the squash on the perforated grill rack and grill, turning, until the squash have browned slightly and are crisp-tender, 6 to 8 minutes total. Transfer the cooked food to the clean baking sheet.

5   Serve hot, with a dollop of the aioli on top of the fish or on the side.

Grilled Salmon Packets with Gingered Slaw

This type of cooking, known as *en papillote*, results in the easiest cleanup of all. Everything cooks in heavy-duty aluminum foil packets on the grill. If you're pressed for time, enlist the grocery store as your sous chef by buying a package of pre-shredded cabbage, as well as shredded carrots and chopped green onions from the salad bar. If you wish, you could serve this dish with cooked ramen or soba noodles instead of rice. Any leftovers become a salmon salad to take to work the next day.

SERVES 4

Gingered Slaw

2 cups finely shredded cabbage

I cup shredded carrots

I cup chopped green onions (white and green parts)

3 tablespoons vegetable oil

3 tablespoons rice vinegar

I tablespoon grated fresh ginger

I teaspoon toasted sesame oil

I tablespoon black sesame seeds (optional)

2 cups cooked rice

Four 5- to 6-ounce salmon fillets or any firm fish fillet

I   Prepare a very hot fire in your grill. You'll want the temperature to be as close to 450°F as you can get it.

2   To make the **Gingered Slaw**, in a large bowl, combine the cabbage, carrots, green onions, vegetable oil, vinegar, ginger, sesame oil, and sesame seeds, if using. Take four 18 x 18-inch sheets of heavy-duty aluminum foil, lay each sheet of foil on a flat surface, and place ¹/₂ cup of cooked rice in the middle. Divide the cabbage mixture among the packets, topping the rice with it.

Place the salmon fillets on top of the slaw. Wrap and seal the foil to form 4 packets.

3 Grill, seam side up, with the grill lid down, for 14 to 16 minutes. Do not turn. To serve, place a packet on each plate, let cool slightly, then open. If you wish, you can transfer the contents to 4 plates and discard the foil or eat right from the foil packet.

TIME-SAVING TIARA TOUCH

The fish packets can be prepared and refrigerated for up to 1 day before grilling, if you wish. The Gingered Slaw is also delicious served raw rather than cooked on the grill.

Grilled Swordfish and Beefsteak Tomatoes with Salsa Verde

The meatiness of swordfish makes it the perfect choice for those who want more fish in their diet, but don't care for more delicate-tasting white fish. The trick to grilling swordfish is to grill it *less* than the 10 minutes per inch of thickness rule of thumb—instead, grill it for 7 to 8 minutes per inch of thickness. This makes all the difference. Pairing this with the grilled tomatoes is a healthy match made in heaven. Serve a crusty loaf of semolina bread on the side to sop up some of the yummy Salsa Verde. Save any leftovers for a grilled swordfish sandwich slathered with Salsa Verde or Quick Aioli (page 192). Or chop up the leftovers, put them over greens, and serve with Lime Vinaigrette (page 198).

SERVES 6

Six 8-ounce swordfish steaks, $^3/_4$ inch thick

6 medium-size beefsteak tomatoes, cut in half

$^1/_2$ cup olive oil

$^1/_4$ cup fresh lemon juice (from about 2 lemons)

Kosher or sea salt and freshly ground black pepper to taste

Salsa Verde

MAKES ABOUT 1 $^3/_4$ CUPS

$^1/_3$ cup finely chopped fresh Italian parsley

$^1/_3$ cup capers, rinsed and finely chopped

6 anchovy fillets, mashed

2 cloves garlic, minced

1 tablespoon Dijon mustard

Juice and zest of 1 lemon, or more to taste

1 cup olive oil

$^1/_8$ teaspoon kosher or sea salt

1   Rinse and pat dry the fish steaks and place in a shallow glass dish. Place the halved tomatoes in another shallow glass dish, cut side up. Combine the olive oil, lemon juice, and salt and pepper. Drizzle over the fish and tomatoes and let them sit at room temperature for 15 to 20 minutes.

2   Prepare a hot fire in your grill.

3   To make the *Salsa Verde*, combine the parsley, capers, anchovies, garlic, mustard, and lemon juice and zest. Slowly whisk in the olive oil, adding the salt and additional lemon juice if necessary. (This can also be made in a food processor: process the parsley, capers, anchovy fillets, garlic, mustard, and lemon juice and zest, then slowly add the oil to make a thick sauce. Stir in the salt.)

4   Grill the swordfish steaks for about 3 minutes per side, depending on the thickness of the fish. Grill the tomatoes, cut side down, alongside the fish steaks for about the same amount of time. To serve, place 2 tomato halves on each plate and lay a tip of the swordfish steak on top of the tomato. Drizzle the salsa over all and serve any additional salsa on the side.

Grilled Tilapia with Avocado-Orange Salad and Lime Vinaigrette

In this very refreshing grilled fish supper, a wonderfully ripe avocado and orange salad is drizzled with a citrus vinaigrette so chock full of herbs that it is almost like a pesto dressing. The grilled tilapia gets a pinch of heat that also pairs well with the splash of lime. We like the Avocado-Orange Salad with grilled chicken, pork, or beef, too. Avocado Salsa Verde (page 106) would also be great with this fish as an alternative.

SERVES 4

Four 6- to 8-ounce tilapia fillets

1 tablespoon olive oil

1 teaspoon red pepper flakes

Fine kosher or sea salt and freshly ground black pepper to taste

Avocado-Orange Salad

One 14-ounce can mandarin oranges, drained

4 cups baby spinach, arugula, or mesclun greens

2 ripe Hass avocados, pitted and sliced

1/4 cup (2 ounces) crumbled blue cheese or feta (optional)

Lime Vinaigrette

MAKES ABOUT 2 CUPS

1 teaspoon lime zest

1 1/2 tablespoons fresh lime juice

2 tablespoons orange juice

1 cup olive oil

4 cloves garlic, minced

1/4 cup chopped fresh Italian parsley

1/2 cup chopped fresh mint or lemon balm leaves

Kosher or sea salt and freshly ground black pepper to taste

You've Got Dinner!

STEAMED RICE, COUSCOUS, OR SOURDOUGH BREAD

1 Rinse the fish fillets and pat dry. Place on a doubled baking sheet, lightly coat with the olive oil, and season with the red pepper flakes, salt, and black pepper.

2 Prepare a hot fire in your grill.

3 While the grill is heating, prepare the *Avocado-Orange Salad*. Place the mandarin oranges in a small bowl of ice cold water to refresh. On each of 4 plates, place 1 cup of the salad greens, half of a sliced avocado, and one-fourth of the drained mandarin oranges. Sprinkle the cheese on top, if using.

4 Combine the *Lime Vinaigrette* ingredients in a large glass jar. Shake vigorously to blend. Immediately spoon about 1 tablespoon of the dressing over just the avocado to keep the avocado from turning brown. (The dressing will keep, tightly covered, in the refrigerator for up to 3 days.)

5 Grill the fish, flesh side down first, for 3 to 4 minutes per side, turning once. Transfer to the clean baking sheet. To serve, place a fish fillet on each plate next to the salad and drizzle additional vinaigrette over the fish and the salad.

TIME-SAVING TIARA TOUCH

Add a few shrimp or scallop skewers to the grill while you're grilling the tilapia, refrigerate in an airtight container, and serve them a day or two later over rice with the leftover Lime Vinaigrette.

Spicy Fish Tacos

The BBQ Queens love fish tacos. They are quick, easy, and perfect for week-nights, serving a family in style, and they're tasty enough for company, too. This recipe is adapted from our cookbook *Fish & Shellfish, Grilled & Smoked* (The Harvard Common Press, 2002). We've made the Lemon Pepper BBQ Rub as simple as can be without forsaking flavor. You'll have leftover rub, so be sure to try some on any other kind of grilled fish or on chicken paillards. For shellfish tacos, try this recipe with either shrimp or scallops. Serve with a crisp beer, such as lager.

MAKES 8 TACOS

Napa Cabbage Slaw

2 cups shredded napa cabbage

I cup assorted baby greens, such as spinach, oak leaf, or Boston lettuce

8 green onions, chopped (white and green parts)

¹/₄ cup tarragon vinegar

¹/₄ cup sour cream (low-fat is okay)

¹/₂ cup fresh lemon juice (from about 4 lemons)

¹/₂ teaspoon fine kosher or sea salt

Lemon Pepper BBQ Rub

MAKES ABOUT ¹/₂ CUP

I¹/₂ tablespoons ground cumin

I¹/₂ tablespoons ground coriander

2 tablespoons lemon pepper

I tablespoon ground chipotle pepper

I tablespoon packed dark brown sugar

You've Got Dinner!

WHITE CORN TORTILLA CHIPS WITH STORE-BOUGHT CORN OR BLACK BEAN SALSA

1½ pounds tilapia, sea bass, or other mild white fish

8 flour tortillas

8 lemon wedges, for garnish

1½ cups salsa of your choice, for garnish

1   Oil the grill grates, then prepare a hot fire in the grill.

2   To make the *Napa Cabbage Slaw*, combine the cabbage, greens, and green onions in a large bowl. In a small bowl, combine the vinegar, sour cream, lemon juice, and salt to make a dressing. Set aside.

3   In another small bowl, combine the *Lemon Pepper BBQ Rub* ingredients. Coat the fish fillets with 4 tablespoons of the rub. Place on a doubled baking sheet and take out to the grill.

4   Grill the fish directly over the flames, flesh side down first, for 4 to 5 minutes per side, or 10 minutes per inch of thickness. Turn only once, halfway through grilling. Remove to the clean baking sheet.

5   Right before assembling the tacos, pour the dressing over the cabbage mixture and toss to blend. To assemble the tacos, place 3 ounces of grilled fish on each tortilla. Top with about ⅓ cup of the cabbage slaw and roll up. Garnish each plate with a lemon wedge and a small ramekin of salsa.

TIME-SAVING TIARA TOUCH

Make a double batch of the Lemon Pepper BBQ Rub and use it on pork chops later in the week.

Garlic-Basil Grilled Trout with Goat Cheese–Stuffed Grilled Tomatoes

Whole trout is a perfect size for the grill. Trout cooked to perfection can be easily deboned. The finished fish needs room on a large plate. Gently lift the tail and loosen the flesh under the tail with a fork. The skeleton should easily lift up off the fish, leaving half a fillet on the plate. Turn the half with the skeleton over. Lift the tail, loosen the flesh underneath, and lift the empty skeleton off the plate and discard. Whole trout makes a great light weeknight dinner because the fish, plus a simple side, is very satisfying. The Garlic-Basil Butter is divine. Make extra to slather on a loaf of French or Italian bread, wrap it in heavy-duty foil, and heat on the grill until browned and crispy.

SERVES 4

Four whole cleaned 12- to 16-ounce rainbow trout

Coarse kosher or sea salt and freshly ground black pepper to taste

2 lemons

4 medium-size beefsteak tomatoes

4 ounces goat cheese or garlic cream cheese

Garlic-Basil Butter
MAKES ABOUT 1 CUP

$^1/_2$ cup (1 stick) unsalted butter

2 cloves garlic, minced

$^1/_2$ cup coarsely chopped fresh basil

$^1/_2$ teaspoon red pepper flakes

$^1/_8$ teaspoon kosher or sea salt

You've Got Dinner!
STEAMED GREEN BEANS OR SPINACH

1 Rinse the trout, pat dry, sprinkle the cavity with salt and pepper, and set on a doubled baking sheet.

2 Cut the lemons in half. Rinse the tomatoes and core out the top so that 1 ounce of goat cheese can be spooned into the indentation of each tomato after grilling. Place the tomatoes and lemons on a separate plate on the baking sheet.

3 Prepare a medium-hot fire in your grill.

4 Meanwhile, to make the *Garlic-Basil Butter*, in a small saucepan, melt the butter, then add the garlic, basil, red pepper, and salt. Stir to blend. Place the pan on the baking sheet with a basting brush and the trout and tomatoes. Carry everything out to the grill.

5 Grill the trout for about 10 to 12 minutes per side, turning once. Brush frequently with the garlic-basil butter inside the cavity and out. Whole trout is done when the thickest, meatiest part begins to flake apart when a fork is inserted.

6 At the same time, set the whole tomatoes on the grill and cook for 12 to 15 minutes. Place the lemon halves cut side down on the grill and cook for 5 to 6 minutes. Remove and place the cooked food on the clean baking sheet. Serve each trout with half a grilled lemon for squeezing over the fish and a whole grilled tomato, with 1 ounce of goat cheese spooned into the indentation.

Spice-Rubbed Tuna Niçoise

This is a great hot weather meal because it's delicious served at room temperature. We suggest you use this recipe as a sort of template, then add other items of your choice. Be creative with what you choose, whether you incorporate "must-use-today" items from your refrigerator, or staples from your pantry, or shop for everything fresh. Here's a short list of additional ingredients you may want to add: boiled or roasted fingerling or new potatoes, grilled or sautéed mushrooms or asparagus, small green beans quickly blanched, Roma or grape tomatoes, and even toasted nuts such as pecans or almonds. Use leftover Spice Rub on other fish fillets, shrimp, or poultry.

SERVES 4

Spice Rub
MAKES ABOUT $^1/_2$ CUP

2 tablespoons sweet paprika

2 tablespoons light or dark brown sugar

I tablespoon ground cumin

I tablespoon ancho chile powder

I tablespoon freshly ground black pepper

I teaspoon fine kosher or sea salt

I teaspoon red pepper flakes

Four 6- to 8-ounce tuna steaks, I inch thick

2 lemons, cut in half

2 limes, cut in half

2 cups mixed salad greens of your choice

8 endive leaves

2 hard-boiled eggs, quartered

I cup pitted oil-cured olives

Two 13.75-ounce cans artichoke hearts (or enough for 8 hearts), drained and cut in half

One 16-ounce jar fire-roasted red peppers, drained

¹/₂ cup store-bought or homemade balsamic vinaigrette

1   Prepare a hot fire in your grill.

2   Combine the *Spice Rub* ingredients in a glass jar. Sprinkle about 1 tablespoon or more of the rub on each tuna steak, then place the tuna on a doubled baking sheet and take out to the grill.

3   Grill the tuna for about 3 minutes per side. (Notice the short cooking time; tuna gets dry if overcooked.) Put the lemons and limes on the grill, cut side down, when you turn the tuna. They will be warmed through when the tuna is cooked.

4   Arrange the salad greens evenly on each of 4 plates. Place the tuna in the center. Arrange the additional ingredients around the tuna. Drizzle with the vinaigrette and encourage diners to squeeze the grilled lemons and limes over all.

TIME-SAVING TIARA TOUCH

Don't forget to look for prewashed bagged mixed salad greens in the grocery store. Instead of buying small cans of artichoke hearts, buy a large jar at a wholesale club. The artichokes keep refrigerated for several months and you'll always have them on hand.

Grilled Walleye with Tangy Red Pepper Sauce and Tapenade-Tossed Linguine

This popular sporting fish is a favorite of Upper Midwestern lake anglers. It has a delicious, sweet, mild flavor. You'll need to use an oiled grill rack so that this fish, which has a delicate texture, won't fall apart on the grill. Our weeknight time-saving tricks for this meal include using store-bought tubes of anchovy paste and black olive or tapenade paste. Cook the pasta first, the pepper sauce next, and then it will take less than 10 minutes to grill the walleye. It's perfectly okay for the pasta to be at room temperature for this dish. Substitute just about any fish fillet for the walleye; even chicken or turkey breasts would be fine to swap. This fish is also good with Asiago Polenta (page 36) instead of the linguine.

SERVES 4

Four 6- to 8-ounce walleye fillets

1 tablespoon olive oil

Fine kosher or sea salt and freshly ground black pepper to taste

1 pound linguine, cooked according to package directions

4 tablespoons extra virgin olive oil

4 tablespoons black olive paste or tapenade

Tangy Red Pepper Sauce

MAKES ABOUT 1 1/2 CUPS

2 tablespoons unsalted butter

One 12-ounce jar roasted red peppers, drained and chopped

2 cloves garlic, minced

2 teaspoons anchovy paste

2 teaspoons capers

1   Place the fish fillets on a doubled baking sheet. Lightly brush with olive oil and season with salt and pepper. Set aside.

2   Place the cooked pasta in a large bowl. Add the olive oil and black olive paste and toss to coat. Cover and set aside.

3   To make the *Tangy Red Pepper Sauce*, melt the butter in a sauté pan over medium-high heat. Add the red peppers, garlic, anchovy paste, and capers. Simmer for 2 to 3 minutes.

4   Prepare a hot fire in your grill. Lightly oil a grill rack on both sides.

5   Place the grill rack on the grill grates. Then place the fish fillets on the grill rack. Grill for 4 minutes on the flesh side, then turn and grill for another 4 minutes, until opaque and just beginning to flake when tested with a fork. Serve topped with the pepper sauce, alongside the linguine.

TIME-SAVING TIARA TOUCH

Keep a variety of dry pastas in your pantry. There are subtle differences in the texture of linguine and fettuccine, for example, and the choice of flat or round pasta will affect how sauces are held. So just by changing your noodle you can create a whole new dish.

Sizzling Shellfish

We have chosen the most readily available and popular shellfish for the grill: shrimp, scallops, lobster, crab, and clams. Who can go wrong with any of these? Well, actually, the person who thinks she needs to grill these delicate creatures well-well-done can go wrong, that's who! So repeat after us: "I shall not overcook my shellfish."

We grill shellfish over high heat quickly. Large shrimp and scallops need only 6 minutes and are done when they *begin* to turn opaque. Clams cook in 3 to 5 minutes and are removed from the grill as soon as they pop open. Lobster tails with the shell on need about 12 minutes. Remember that just like meat, shellfish keep cooking after they leave the grill. And we want to spare you the culinary agony of tough, dry seafood.

For weeknight grilling, purchase peeled and deveined shrimp. This alone will save you anywhere from 15 to 30 minutes of prep time. Also, cook more than you need so you can make one of our leftover recipes, such as Venetian Grilled Shrimp Soup (page 230), Low Country Black-Eyed Pea and Grilled Jumbo Shrimp Salad with Hot

Bacon Dressing (page 62), or Grilled Lobster Potato Cakes with White Wine Lemon Drizzle and Mache (page 216). Grilled shrimp and scallops can be added to a number of other wonderful salads, including the quintessential Caesar and Cobb salads, or can be chopped and whipped together with a bit of mayonnaise or plain yogurt to stuff an avocado half.

Our favorite gadgets for grilling shellfish are the grill wok and the perforated grill rack. These handy gadgets will keep the small critters from falling through the grill grates into the fire. After all, you want to enjoy every delicious morsel!

Clambake on the Grill!

The popularity of clambakes in New England and fish boils in Wisconsin all point to how good seafood tastes when cooked outdoors. In this recipe, the traditional clams, potatoes, and corn are all grilled and slathered with a yummy citrus butter with a hint of smoke, with much less fuss than a regular beachside clambake. And the cleanup is a snap! Don't forget to add a good brewski. You could also substitute mussels for the clams if you wish. Do not be afraid of liquid smoke: it is a natural product, made from real wood smoke.

SERVES 4

Smoky Citrus Butter
MAKES ABOUT 1 1/4 CUPS

1 cup (2 sticks) unsalted butter

Juice and zest of 1 lemon

2 teaspoons liquid smoke flavoring

1 pound new potatoes

2 pounds fresh hard-shell clams, well scrubbed

4 ears fresh corn, husks and silks removed

You've Got Dinner!
A GREEN SALAD AND A HUNK OF BREAD

1   To make the *Smoky Citrus Butter*, melt the butter in a small saucepan over medium heat. Stir in the lemon juice and zest and the smoke flavoring. Set aside, keeping warm.

2   Prepare a hot fire in your grill.

3   Prick the potatoes all over with a fork or paring knife and microwave on high for 4 minutes, or until cooked halfway through. Rinse the clams well and discard any that are partially opened. Place the clams in large plastic bags. Place the potatoes, corn, bags of clams, and smoky citrus butter on a baking sheet and take out to the grill.

4 Brush the potatoes and corn with some of the butter and grill for 1 to 2 minutes per side, or until browned and tender. Transfer to the baking tray. Remove the clams from the bags and place them on the grill. Close the lid and grill for 3 to 5 minutes, or until the clams have opened. (Discard any clams that have not opened.) Transfer to the baking sheet and drizzle with butter. Arrange the clams, potatoes, and corn on a large serving platter or on individual plates. Pass the remaining butter at the table for dipping.

Grilled Crab Cakes and Broccolini with Seasoned Lemon Butter

Crab cakes are often made with egg to help bind the meat together. But mayonnaise and mustard do the trick quite nicely, and using this method you won't have to worry about overcooking the crab in order to cook the egg all the way through. You'll need a grill rack so that the precious crabmeat doesn't fall through the grill grates. Broccolini is a cross between Chinese kale and broccoli. Its stalks are thinner than those of broccoli and it has a nice sweet flavor. It grills beautifully.

SERVES 2

I pound fresh lump crabmeat, picked clean of shells and cartilage

I cup crushed saltine crackers

8 green onions (green and white parts), finely chopped

$^1/_4$ cup chopped roasted red peppers

3 tablespoons regular or low-fat mayonnaise

3 tablespoons Dijon mustard

I teaspoon fresh lemon juice

Kosher or sea salt and lemon pepper to taste

8 ounces broccolini, ends trimmed and separated into stalks

2 tablespoons olive oil

Seasoned Lemon Butter

MAKES ABOUT $^1/_2$ CUP

$^1/_2$ cup (I stick) unsalted butter

Zest and juice of I lemon

I teaspoon seasoned pepper or other spice rub of your choice

4 slices sourdough bread, grilled or toasted

1 In a large bowl, combine the crabmeat, crushed crackers, green onions, red peppers, mayonnaise, mustard, lemon juice, and salt and pepper. Gently combine and form four 1-inch-thick cakes. Set on a plate, cover, and refrigerate for 15 minutes.

2 Place the broccolini on a baking sheet and drizzle with olive oil. Set aside.

3 Prepare a hot fire in your grill. Lightly oil both sides of a grill rack and place over the fire.

4 To make the **Seasoned Lemon Butter**, melt the butter in a small saucepan. Add the lemon zest and juice and the seasoned pepper. Blend and keep warm over low heat.

5 Grill the crab cakes on the grill rack for 3 to 4 minutes per side, turning once. At the same time, grill the broccolini (with the florets away from the intense side of the fire) for 4 to 5 minutes, turning once halfway through the cooking time.

6 Serve the crab cakes over a piece of sourdough toast, with the broccolini spears on the side. Drizzle everything with the lemon butter.

Star Anise–Buttered Lobster Tails with Smashed Parsley Potatoes

Sometimes it's good to splurge during the week. Treat yourselves like company and prepare these fabulous lobster tails on the grill. Serve with smashed potatoes (our rustic recipe for slightly lumpy mashed potatoes) and salad. If you like, substitute 1 teaspoon dried tarragon or 1 tablespoon chopped fresh basil or parsley in place of the star anise. Leftover grilled lobster or shrimp coarsely chopped and mixed with leftover smashed potatoes make exquisite potato pancakes (see page 216). Hint, hint: cook and grill for leftovers!

MAKES 4 SERVINGS

Four 8-ounce uncooked rock lobster tails, in their shells

1 tablespoon extra virgin olive oil

6 medium-size red potatoes

2 tablespoons chopped fresh Italian parsley

2 tablespoons unsalted butter

Star Anise Butter

MAKES ABOUT ²/₃ CUP

¹/₂ cup (1 stick) unsalted butter

Zest and juice of 1 lemon

2 whole star anise

2 tablespoons chopped fresh tarragon leaves

You've Got Dinner!

BUTTER LETTUCE SALAD WITH ARTICHOKE HEARTS AND ROASTED RED PEPPERS

1   Cut the top membrane from the lobster tails and discard. Loosen the meat within the shell and brush the shell with the olive oil.

2   In a large saucepan, add the potatoes and just barely cover with cold water. Cook over high heat for 20 to 25 minutes. When fork tender, drain the water. Smash the potatoes, skin and all, just a few times. They should still

be a bit lumpy. Add the parsley and butter and stir to combine. Cover and set aside.

3 Prepare a hot fire in your grill.

4 Meanwhile, to make the **Star Anise Butter**, in a small saucepan over medium heat, melt the butter, then add the lemon zest and juice, star anise, and chopped tarragon. Stir to blend. Cover and keep warm over low heat.

5 Place the lobster tails on the grill, cut side down, and grill for 2 to 3 minutes. Turn the tails and grill until done, 7 to 9 minutes total. The shell may char, but the meat should be an opaque white. Cover the grill for speedier cooking, but do not overcook the lobster or it will be rubbery.

6 Spoon 1 or 2 tablespoons of the star anise butter into the smashed potatoes and stir to blend. Serve the lobster tails and smashed potatoes with the remaining star anise butter on the side for drizzling or dipping.

Grilled Lobster Potato Cakes with White Wine Lemon Drizzle and Mache

Take a look at the Star Anise–Buttered Lobster Tails recipe (page 214) and you'll see where this recipe is coming from. But even without that, potato pancakes have been a favorite of BBQ Queens everywhere. Judith lived in London for a couple of years, where potato and fish cakes are sometimes thought of as "pub fare." Karen remembers thinner, but just as delicious, white fish and potato pancakes served in a lemon champagne sauce from one of her visits to Willi's Wine Bar in Paris. So this is our take on using leftover grilled shellfish, preferably shrimp or lobster, but you can use any leftover fish for this recipe, too. If you have leftover (s)mashed potatoes, then you can skip the part about cooking the potatoes. We're adding another bit of European flair by including mache salad. Mache is a leafy green also known as lamb's lettuce or corn salad; rinse it well, because it tends to be gritty. Warm crusty bread on the side is a must for sopping up every bit of the sauce. And don't forget to serve the remaining white wine!

SERVES 4

6 medium-size red potatoes

Two 8-ounce grilled rock lobster tails or I pound grilled shrimp

White Wine Lemon Drizzle
MAKES ABOUT I CUP

$^1/_2$ cup (I stick) unsalted butter

$^1/_3$ cup dry white wine

Zest and juice of I lemon

3 tablespoons chopped fresh Italian parsley

1 cup flour mixed with 1 teaspoon salt and 1 teaspoon freshly ground black pepper, for dusting the pancakes

$^1/_4$ cup olive oil

$^1/_4$ cup ($^1/_2$ stick) unsalted butter

2 cups mache

1   In a large saucepan, add the potatoes and just barely cover with cold water. Cook over high heat for 20 to 25 minutes. When fork tender, drain the water. Smash the potatoes, skin and all, a few times with a potato masher. They should still be a bit lumpy. Cover and set aside.

2   Coarsely chop the grilled shellfish and set aside.

3   To make the *White Wine Lemon Drizzle*, melt the butter in a small saucepan over medium heat. Stir in the wine, lemon zest and juice, and parsley. Keep warm over low heat.

4   Spoon 3 or 4 tablespoons of the lemon drizzle into the smashed potatoes. The potatoes should be soft enough to just stir. Stir in the chopped shellfish. Using your hands, form 8 potato pancakes and dust in the seasoned flour to keep the pancakes from being too sticky. Place the pancakes on a plate.

5   In a large sauté pan, heat half of the olive oil and half of the butter over medium-high heat. Place 4 potato pancakes in the pan and sauté until light golden brown on each side, turning only once, 8 to 10 minutes. Keep warm in a low oven while you heat the remaining olive oil and butter and cook the remaining 4 pancakes.

6   Divide the mache evenly among 4 dinner plates. Top each salad with 2 pancakes. Spoon the lemon drizzle over the pancakes and the mache and serve hot.

Chopsticks Spot Prawns and Summer Vegetable Skewers with Gingered Teriyaki Glaze

Alaska spot prawns are so big and so luscious that they deserve a signature style. In this recipe, they are threaded onto bamboo "chopstick" skewers, although you can use any kind of skewer you like. The word "teriyaki" is a combination of the Japanese words *teri*, meaning "luster," and *yaki*, meaning "grill" or "broil." In a teriyaki dish, ingredients are cooked over high heat after being marinated in or basted with teriyaki sauce, which gives the luster or shine to the food.

SERVES 4

Gingered Teriyaki Glaze
MAKES ABOUT $^3/_4$ CUP

> 2 teaspoons finely grated fresh ginger
>
> $^1/_2$ cup store-bought teriyaki sauce of your choice
>
> $^1/_4$ cup vegetable oil
>
> 12 Alaska spot prawns or the largest raw shrimp you can find, peeled and deveined
>
> 8 wooden skewers, soaked in water for at least 30 minutes prior to grilling
>
> 2 Japanese eggplants, cut into 2-inch pieces
>
> 1 medium-size red bell pepper, cut into 2-inch pieces
>
> 15 green onions

You've Got Dinner!
CELLOPHANE NOODLES OR STEAMED RICE

1 To make the *Gingered Teriyaki Glaze*, in a small bowl, mix the ginger, teriyaki sauce, and vegetable oil together. Divide the glaze in half.

2   Place 3 spot prawns on each of 4 skewers, piercing through both the head and the tail of each shrimp. Alternate the eggplant and red bell pepper pieces on the remaining 4 skewers. Brush the vegetables, then each shrimp, with half of the teriyaki glaze and place each skewer on a doubled baking sheet to marinate for 30 minutes. Reserve the remaining glaze.

3   Prepare a hot fire in your grill.

4   Grill each skewer for 4 to 5 minutes per side, brushing with the remaining glaze, or until the prawns turn pink and are opaque all the way through and the vegetables have good grill marks. Grill the green onions, placed perpendicular to the grill grates, for 2 to 3 minutes per side, or until they have good grill marks. Remove the cooked food to a clean baking sheet. Serve hot.

Pistachio-Scallion Sea Scallops with Sugar Snap Peas and Teardrop Tomatoes

We love sea scallops seared over a hot fire. They cook quickly and are a great choice for a fast but fancy weeknight dinner. The scallops need to grill on a pre-oiled, hot grill rack. At the same time that they are cooking, the sugar snap peas and tomatoes grill alongside in a grill wok. Sugar snap peas are fresh in the spring, so if you plan to make this dinner in the summer, substitute green beans, broccoli, or green bell peppers. Also feel free to substitute shrimp, farm-raised catfish fillets, salmon, trout, or any other white fish for the scallops. Between the vegetable choices and the fish choices, you can make this quite often and no one will be the wiser!

SERVES 4

2 pounds large sea scallops

1 pound sugar snap peas, stems removed

2 cups (1 pint) yellow teardrop tomatoes

Pistachio-Scallion Butter

MAKES ABOUT ²/₃ CUP

¹/₂ cup (1 stick) unsalted butter

2 tablespoons chopped natural pistachios

2 tablespoons chopped scallions (white and green parts)

Zest and juice from 1 lime

¹/₄ teaspoon fine kosher or sea salt

¹/₂ teaspoon hot pepper sauce, or to your taste

You've Got Dinner!
COUSCOUS, ORZO, OR STEAMED RICE

1   Rinse the scallops, pat dry, and place on a plate. Set aside.

2   Place the snap peas and tomatoes in an oiled grill wok. Place the wok on a baking sheet. Place the plate of scallops on the baking sheet.

3   In a small saucepan, combine the *Pistachio-Scallion Butter* ingredients and cook over medium heat for 4 to 5 minutes. Remove from the heat. Pour 2 tablespoons into a ramekin to use on the raw scallops while grilling. Reserve the rest, keeping warm over low heat, to drizzle over the cooked food.

4   Prepare a hot fire in your grill. Oil a perforated grill rack on both sides and place on the grill grate.

5   Brush the sea scallops with the 2 tablespoons of pistachio-scallion butter and place on the oiled perforated grill rack. Grill for about 3 minutes before turning. If the scallops stick, cook them a little longer, until they turn easily. After turning, baste and grill long enough to heat through, 1 to 2 minutes.

6   At the same time, place the grill wok containing the sugar snap peas and tomatoes on the grill beside the scallops. Toss the vegetables several times, using wooden paddles or grill spatulas. When you remove the scallops from the grill, place the cover on the grill for 1 to 2 more minutes to heat the vegetables all the way through.

7   Serve the grilled scallops on top of the sugar snap peas and tomatoes. Drizzle all with the reserved pistachio-scallion butter.

Sesame-Soy Stir-Grilled Shrimp, Snow Peas, Yellow Peppers, and Cherry Tomatoes

This is the BBQ Queens' favorite grill wok recipe. It combines texture, color, and taste at its best. The ingredients are straightforward and easy to find, the shrimp and the vegetables all cook quickly, and it is one entire meal. The rice takes about 30 minutes to cook, so get that started first. Instead of the shrimp, you could also use chicken breast, salmon, or scallops.

SERVES 4

I pound medium-size to large shrimp, peeled and deveined

$^1/_2$ pound snow peas, stems removed

I medium-size yellow pepper, stemmed, seeded, and cut into $^1/_4$-inch strips

2 cups (I pint) cherry tomatoes

$^1/_2$ large red onion, sliced into $^1/_4$-inch wedges

Sweet and Spicy Soy Marinade
MAKES ABOUT $^2/_3$ CUP

$^1/_4$ cup soy sauce

$^1/_4$ cup rice vinegar

2 tablespoons honey

4 cloves garlic, minced

I teaspoon freshly grated ginger

I teaspoon toasted sesame oil

I $^1/_2$ cups cooked rice

1   Place the shrimp, snow peas, pepper, tomatoes, and red onion in a large zipper-top plastic bag.

2   Combine the *Sweet and Spicy Soy Marinade* ingredients in a small bowl. Pour the marinade over the shrimp and vegetables. Seal the bag and toss to coat. Marinate for about 20 minutes at room temperature.

3   Prepare a hot fire in your grill. Oil a grill wok on both sides.

4   Pour the shrimp mixture into the oiled grill wok over the kitchen sink to drain the liquid. Place the wok on a doubled baking sheet and carry out to the grill. Place the wok on the grill and stir-grill the shrimp and vegetables, tossing with wooden paddles or grill spatulas, for 6 to 8 minutes. Move the wok to the indirect side of the grill. Close the lid on the grill and cook for another 4 to 5 minutes (longer if it is cold outside). Remove the wok to the clean baking sheet.

5   Divide the rice among 4 dinner plates and top with one-fourth of the shrimp and vegetables. Serve immediately.

TIME-SAVING TIARA TOUCH

We like to buy fresh or frozen raw shrimp already peeled and deveined as a great time-saver for a weeknight meal.

Wood-Grilled Shrimp Cocktail

Shrimp are festive and special, and more available and affordable than ever. Remember the first shrimp cocktail you ordered at a restaurant? We sure do! So let's take it to another level. Instead of boiling the shrimp, we'll prepare them on the grill and add a bit of wood to the fire for a sublime smokiness. Toss 1 cup of wood chips (soaked in water for 30 minutes) directly onto a charcoal fire, or put dry wood chips in a foil packet poked with holes and place on the grill grate over the burner in a gas grill. Or if you don't want to bother with soaking the wood chips, use $1/3$ cup dry flavored wood pellets in a foil packet poked with holes for either charcoal or gas grills.

SERVES 4

BBQ Cocktail Sauce
MAKES ABOUT 1 CUP

1 cup store-bought chili sauce of your choice

$1/2$ cup store-bought chunky salsa of your choice

$1/2$ cup store-bought spicy barbecue sauce of your choice

1 tablespoon horseradish

Zest and juice of 1 lemon

1 teaspoon hot sauce

2 pounds large shrimp, peeled and deveined

$1/2$ cup store-bought or homemade Italian salad dressing

$1/4$ cup spicy barbecue sauce

4 ears fresh corn, husks and silks removed

1 tablespoon olive oil

Fine kosher or sea salt to taste

1 cup wood chips or $1/3$ cup wood pellets (the **BBQ Queens** suggest apple, hickory, oak, or pecan; see above)

1 lemon, cut into quarters

1 lime, cut into quarters

You've Got Dinner!
STEAMED NEW POTATOES, POTATO SALAD, OR PACKET POTATOES (SEE PAGE 98)

1 Combine the **BBQ Cocktail Sauce** ingredients in a medium-size bowl. Stir to blend, cover, and chill in the refrigerator until ready to serve. Combine the shrimp, Italian dressing, and barbecue sauce in a large bowl and set aside to marinate for 15 to 30 minutes.

2 Rub each ear of corn with ¼ tablespoon of olive oil. Lightly salt each ear. Set on a plate.

3 Prepare a hot fire in your grill. Lightly oil a large grill wok and set aside. For a gas grill, immediately place a packet of dry chips or pellets on the grill grate toward the back of the grill and close the lid. The chips will begin to smoke after 20 minutes. For a charcoal fire, sprinkle moistened wood chips or place a foil packet containing dry wood pellets on the hot coals right before grilling.

4 Place the shrimp in a grill wok and drain over the kitchen sink. Place the wok and plate of corn on a doubled baking sheet and carry out to the grill. Grill the shrimp in the wok, stirring often with wooden paddles or grill spatulas, for 7 to 8 minutes, or until the shrimp are pink, firm, and opaque. Place the corn on the grill grates, turning each ear to get the corn a little charred all over, and grill for 5 to 7 minutes. Remove the cooked food to the clean baking sheet.

5 Spoon the chilled cocktail sauce into 4 individual ramekins. Place an ear of corn on each dinner plate. Serve the shrimp on a big platter, family style, with the lemon and lime wedges.

TIME-SAVING TIARA TOUCH

If you have a larger grill, double the amount of shrimp you grill for this recipe and use the leftovers later in the week for Wood-Grilled Shrimp Quesadillas (page 226).

Wood-Grilled Shrimp Quesadillas

Here's another super-fast déjà vu dinner, made possible by leftovers. Shrimp are so versatile—you can toss them into a salad, or serve them over pasta, Spanish-style rice, or pilaf, or serve them with baguette slices for fancy but easy hors d'oeuvres. Try these quesadillas for a casual dinner along with a romaine salad tossed with the Italian Salsa Vinaigrette.

SERVES 4

2 pounds large grilled shrimp, whole or chopped according to your preference

8 flour tortillas

2 cups chopped green onions (white and green parts)

I cup canned black beans, rinsed and drained

I cup shredded Monterey Jack cheese

I cup shredded *queso fresco* or cheddar cheese

Italian Salsa Vinaigrette

MAKES $^1/_2$ CUP

$^1/_4$ cup Italian salad dressing of your choice

$^1/_4$ cup salsa

I head romaine lettuce, torn into bite-size pieces

Sour cream for garnish

Guacamole for garnish

Salsa for garnish

You've Got Dinner!

STEAMED GREEN BEANS OR BROCCOLI OR SAUTÉED YELLOW SUMMER SQUASH

I   Preheat the oven to 350°F.

2   Place a few shrimp on a flour tortilla and top with $^1/_2$ cup of the chopped green onions, $^1/_4$ cup of the black beans, and $^1/_4$ cup of each of the grated cheeses. Place another tortilla on top and place on a baking sheet. Repeat

with the rest of the tortillas. Bake in the oven until the cheese melts, 10 to 15 minutes.

3   To make the *Italian Salsa Vinaigrette*, combine the Italian dressing and the salsa in a glass jar with a tight-fitting lid and shake to blend.

4   In a large bowl, toss the lettuce with the salsa vinaigrette. Serve as a side with the quesadillas, along with the sour cream, guacamole, and salsa.

TIME-SAVING TIARA TOUCH

You can easily make your own simple version of guacamole by mashing ripe avocados together with chopped red onions, cilantro, and lime juice, but keep in mind that fresh guacamole is readily available in many supermarkets these days. Look in the produce or deli section.

Lime-Basil Shrimp with Grilled Polenta and Asparagus

What an easy meal to assemble while the grill is heating up! It also offers the benefit of aromatherapy, with the heavenly scents of fresh lemon and basil. Frozen and thawed, peeled and deveined shrimp are fine to use for this dish— just place them in the refrigerator in the morning to thaw before dinner. You can find prepared polenta in the produce section of your supermarket. We like to serve this family style on a big platter, with the grilled polenta on the bottom, the shrimp mounded in the middle, and the asparagus spears around the perimeter, but do whatever is easiest for you. It will all taste wonderful no matter how you serve it up. Grill extra shrimp, if you wish, for leftovers.

SERVES 4

Lime-Basil Baste
MAKES ABOUT 1 ¹/₄ CUPS

2 large cloves garlic, minced

2 teaspoons Dijon mustard

¹/₃ cup dry white wine

¹/₄ cup fresh lime juice

¹/₂ cup olive oil

¹/₃ cup chopped fresh basil leaves

Kosher or sea salt and freshly ground black pepper to taste

1¹/₄ pounds (about 24) jumbo or large shrimp, peeled and deveined

1 pound asparagus, ends trimmed

1 pound store-bought prepared polenta, cut into 1-inch-thick slices

1 Combine the *Lime-Basil Baste* ingredients in a medium-size bowl. Pour ¹/₂ cup of the mixture into a large zipper-top plastic bag and add the shrimp.

Seal the bag, toss the shrimp with the baste, and let marinate in the refrigerator for 15 to 20 minutes. Reserve the remaining ¾ cup of baste.

2 Meanwhile, prepare a hot fire in your grill. Oil a perforated grill rack and set aside.

3 Place the shrimp, asparagus, polenta, and remaining lime-basil baste on a baking sheet and take out to the grill. Brush the asparagus and polenta with the baste and grill for 2 to 3 minutes per side, turning once, until browned and slightly charred. Place the grill rack on the grill and place the shrimp on the grill rack, using a slotted spoon to remove them from the bag. Grill for 5 minutes, turning several times, until the shrimp turn pink and opaque. Arrange the polenta, asparagus, and shrimp on a platter and drizzle with any remaining baste. Serve immediately.

Venetian Grilled Shrimp Soup

Imagine you're in a gondola, gliding through the canals of Venice as the sun sets. We'd be lying to you if we told you this heady stew was as relaxing as a gondola ride, but really, it's not that far behind. Grilling the shrimp and bread, then adding them at the last minute to the soup, gives you a punch of flavor you wouldn't get otherwise. If you're already at the grill, why not take the opportunity to plan ahead and also grill a couple of chicken breasts for use later in the week? As a matter of fact, you could use grilled chicken in this soup instead of shrimp. Or try ham, pork, or beef. Serve this soup with more grilled bread, if you like, and fresh fruit salad, or *macedonia*, as those Venetians would call it.

SERVES 4

16 large shrimp, peeled and deveined

3 tablespoons olive oil, plus more for brushing

2 tablespoons fresh lemon juice

I tablespoon Dijon mustard

8 cloves garlic, finely chopped

I teaspoon dried oregano

8 cups store-bought or homemade chicken broth

2 cups canned cannellini beans, rinsed and drained

2 cups chopped canned tomatoes

4 thick slices French or Italian bread

Fine kosher or sea salt and freshly ground black pepper to taste

4 teaspoons extra virgin olive oil, for garnish

4 tablespoons minced fresh Italian parsley and/or basil, for garnish

I   Place the shrimp in a large zipper-top plastic bag. Add 2 tablespoons of the olive oil, the lemon juice, and the Dijon mustard, seal the bag, toss to coat, and marinate in the refrigerator for about 15 minutes.

2 In the meantime, prepare a hot fire in your grill.

3 Heat the remaining 1 tablespoon of olive oil over medium heat in a large pot or Dutch oven. Add the garlic and cook, stirring, until it is golden brown. Add the oregano and stir to blend. Add the chicken broth, beans, and tomatoes. Place the raw shrimp on a plate and pour the marinade into the pot of soup. Simmer over medium heat while you grill the shrimp.

4 Brush both sides of the bread with olive oil. Place the plate of shrimp and bread on a baking sheet and take out to the grill.

5 Grill the shrimp and bread for about 3 minutes, turning once. Remove to the clean baking sheet. Add the shrimp to the soup and simmer for another 3 to 4 minutes. Season with salt and pepper.

6 Place a piece of grilled bread in the bottom of 4 soup bowls. Ladle the soup into each bowl, making sure that each bowl receives equal amounts of beans and shrimp. Drizzle 1 teaspoon of the extra virgin olive oil over each bowl of soup and garnish each with 1 tablespoon of the parsley and/or basil. Serve immediately.

Stuffed Grilled Squid with Boursin and Herbs

The mildly savory stuffing keeps the squid moist and tender during the quick grilling process. The simple secret to cooking tender squid is to cook it either super fast or for a very long time. Since this is a book about weeknight dinners, this recipe calls for cooking it super fast! This is a favorite seaside summer meal for the BBQ Queens, because it makes us think of the Mediterranean. So plan the rest of the meal with that in mind. Start with a bowl of mixed olives with a squeeze of fresh lemon juice.

SERVES 4

$^1/_3$ cup freshly snipped chives

$^1/_2$ cup fine dry bread crumbs

2 cloves garlic, minced

$^1/_2$ cup cream cheese, at room temperature

$^1/_4$ cup (2 ounces) crumbled blue cheese

Kosher or sea salt and freshly ground black pepper to taste

8 medium-size whole squid (6 to 8 inches long), cleaned

$^1/_4$ cup olive oil

You've Got Dinner!

PASTA SALAD WITH CHOPPED TOMATOES AND CUCUMBERS TOSSED WITH VINAIGRETTE

1   Prepare a hot fire in your grill.

2   In a medium-size bowl, mix together the chives, bread crumbs, garlic, cheeses, salt, and pepper. Place the squid on a flat surface and open the body cavity. Stuff the cavity of each squid with the cheese mixture. Pin the cavity closed with toothpicks. Brush the squid all over with the olive oil and place on an oiled perforated grill rack or in hinged grill baskets.

3   Grill the squid until the exterior is slightly charred, the squid is opaque, and the stuffing has warmed through, 2 to 3 minutes per side. Serve hot.

TIME-SAVING TIARA TOUCH

If all you can find at your fishmonger's is whole uncleaned squid, ask the person behind the counter to clean it for you; he or she will be happy to oblige.

Measurement Equivalents

Please note that all conversions are approximate.

Liquid Conversions			Weight Conversions			Oven Temperature Conversions		
U.S.	**Metric**		**U.S./U.K.**	**Metric**		**°F**	**Gas Mark**	**°C**
1 tsp	5 ml		$^1/_2$ oz	14 g		250	$^1/_2$	120
1 tbs	15 ml		1 oz	28 g		275	1	140
2 tbs	30 ml		1$^1/_2$ oz	43 g		300	2	150
3 tbs	45 ml		2 oz	57 g		325	3	165
$^1/_4$ cup	60 ml		2$^1/_2$ oz	71 g		350	4	180
$^1/_3$ cup	75 ml		3 oz	85 g		375	5	190
$^1/_3$ cup + 1 tbs	90 ml		3$^1/_2$ oz	100 g		400	6	200
$^1/_3$ cup + 2 tbs	100 ml		4 oz	113 g		425	7	220
$^1/_2$ cup	120 ml		5 oz	142 g		450	8	230
$^2/_3$ cup	150 ml		6 oz	170 g		475	9	240
$^3/_4$ cup	180 ml		7 oz	200 g		500	10	260
$^3/_4$ cup + 2 tbs	200 ml		8 oz	227 g		550	Broil	290
1 cup	240 ml		9 oz	255 g				
1 cup + 2 tbs	275 ml		10 oz	284 g				
1$^1/_4$ cups	300 ml		11 oz	312 g				
1$^1/_3$ cups	325 ml		12 oz	340 g				
1$^1/_2$ cups	350 ml		13 oz	368 g				
1$^2/_3$ cups	375 ml		14 oz	400 g				
1$^3/_4$ cups	400 ml		15 oz	425 g				
1$^3/_4$ cups + 2 tbs	450 ml		1 lb	454 g				
2 cups (1 pint)	475 ml							
2$^1/_2$ cups	600 ml							
3 cups	720 ml							
4 cups (1 quart)	945 ml (1,000 ml is 1 liter)							

Index